Muslim *Baradaries*, Occupations and Education

Muslim *Baradaries*, Occupations and Education

Abdul Waheed

Centre for Promotion of Educational and Cultural
Advancement of Muslims of India (CEPECAMI)
Aligarh Muslim University, Aligarh

SERIALS PUBLICATIONS
NEW DELHI (INDIA)

First Published – 2011

ISBN: 978-81-8387-458-8

Published by

SERIALS PUBLICATIONS
4830/24, 1st Floor, Ansari Road
Darya Ganj, New Delhi-110002 (India)
Phone : 23245225. Fax : 91-11-23272135
E-mail : serials@sify.com
serialspublications.india@gmail.com
Website: www.serialspublications.com

Contents

Preface

A quarter century back Dr. Gopal Singh, Chairman of High Level Committee (HLC), set up by Ministry of Home Affairs, Govt. of India in early 1980 to enquire into the condition of religious minorities, Scheduled Castes (SCs) and Scheduled Tribes (STs), highlighted serious problem of non-availability of data about socio-economic and educational condition of minorities in following words:

> "No data was available in any public office as to the benefits accruing to the vast religious minorities (now numbering about 120 million) as none were specifically earmarked for them (as they were indeed for the Schedule Castes and Schedule Tribes). No data could be made available to us by the Minorities' Commission (established by a previous government in 1978), which had the necessary authority and the infrastructure to hold such an enquiry. The Universities (including the Muslim Universities) and various social welfare organizations whom we contacted had also no relevant material with them, nor the census report threw any light whatsoever, on the subject of our enquiry. (Even the population figures of the Minorities collected at the 1981 census were not made available to us in spite of our best efforts). Against the employment exchanges, they were bitter and large-scale complaints that they did not even register the names of the Minorities, let alone offer them any openings. Distinguished public men and legislators, including Members of Parliament, whom we contacted personally or through correspondence, could not help us out with any factual data, either. Complaints were mostly built on hearsay and emotion rather than hard facts and reasoned arguments. Solutions were suggested to us, which would, in our opinion, only aggravate the problem". (GoI, 1983: V)

The problem still persists and is rightly highlighted by Prime Minister's High Level Committee (PHLC), constituted under the chairmanship of retired Justice Rajinder Sachar to prepare a report on social, economic and educational status of Muslims in 2005. While emphasizing upon the necessity and significance of detailed data for transparency, and good governance, PHLC Report clearly states:

> "The Committee had faced the acute problem of non-availability of reliable data and, therefore, had to launch an independent effort to collect, collate and, consolidate available data. The data obtained through these mechanisms with considerable difficulty was still not exhaustive enough to analyse several issues to our satisfaction. There is an immediate need, therefore, to make arrangements to collect data for different Socio-Religious Communities (SRCs) on a regular basis and make it available to researchers and the public." (GoI, 2006: 238)

Furthermore, the Report categorically points out that:

> "The Census, the National Accounts Statistics (NAS) and National Sample Survey Organization (NSSO) are the most important sources of large scale good quality data but they are not able to readily provide data on crucial variables to assess the social, economic and educational conditions according to SRCs. There is an urgent need, therefore, to assess afresh the data needs for evaluating conditions of citizens by SRC status on a regular basis so as to understand and assess the flow of development benefits." (Ibid: 238)

Hence PHLC recommends for the "creation of a National Data Bank (NDB) where all relevant data for various SRCs are maintained. All the data should be eventually computerized and made available on the Internet." (Ibid: 238)

Up till now Govt. of India has neither created NDB nor made it binding on its data collecting agencies to classify data according to SRCs and make it public. Obviously, non-availability of detailed data make it difficult to understand problems of communities in right perspective and make effective policies for their welfare and empowerment.

This baseline household survey is a humble effort to generate data about socio-economic and educational condition of Muslims in *Tehsil Koil,* district Aligarh, Uttar Pradesh. A sample of 2500 Muslim households -1000 from nine villages and 1500 from 12 localities of 3 urban agglomeration - was drawn for the survey, conducted in May-June 2007. The report of the survey is divided into 6 chapters barring Introduction and Conclusion.

A brief account of the district as well as localities of the survey and its methodology is presented in Chapter-I whereas data pertaining to basic household amenities and population characteristics are explained in Chapter-II. Chapter-III provides information about *baradaries* (caste-like groups) and their administrative classification into General and Other Backward Classes (OBCs). Also level of awareness among Respondents about administrative status of their *baradaries* is explored and presented in this chapter. Work Participation Rate (WPR) of the population, occupations of workers and their income can be seen in Chapter-IV which also exhibits income disparity between rural-urban and General-OBC workers. Next is the Chapter devoted to explain rate of literacy as well as level of traditional, modern and professional/technical education across rural-urban, General-OBC and gender categories. A survey of 89 neighbourhood schools and 34 Madaris was carried out along with household survey to find out the level of school education and its quality available to Muslim children. Data of this survey is presented in the last Chapter.

The survey was conducted under the auspices of Centre for Promotion of Educational and Cultural Advancement of Muslims of India (CEPECAMI), established in 1988 under section 5(2) (c) of AMU Amendment Act 1981. Needless to say that one of the aims of CEPECAMI is to generate data about the status of Indian Muslims. We do hope this report of the survey could be of immense benefit to social activists, policy makers and researchers.

This survey could not be completed without the permission of the then Vice-Chancellor of the university, Mr. Nasim

Ahmad and the financial support by the Ministry of HRD, Government of India. I am highly grateful to Prof. P.K. Abdul Azis, incumbent Vice-Chancellor of the university for granting the permission to publish survey report. Mr. Gyanendra Mishra, Research Scholar, Dept. of Sociology and Social Work, AMU Aligarh who worked as Research Assistant in the project deserves to be praised for his intelligent intervention, meticulous work and sincere commitment. I am highly indebted to Dr. Mohammad Shahid, Assistant Professor, Social Work, Ambedkar College, Delhi University who voluntarily rendered his services for making the design of the survey, formulation of the questionnaire, interpretation of data etc. I would be failing in my duty if I do not acknowledge hospitality of Respondents and Informants as well as assistance of 21 Field Investigators who were Research Scholars of AMU, Mr. Santosh Varshney who developed Software for data analysis and the Office Staff of CEPECAMI, Mr. S.M. Qamar Alam, Mr. S. Amir Kamal, Mr. Wasim Haider and Raise Ahmad.

29th September, 2010 **Dr. Abdul Waheed**

1

Setting and Design of the Survey

District Aligarh: A Profile

Aligarh is one of the seventy-one districts of Uttar Pradesh, the most populous and socio-politically significant State of India. It lies in western region of the State and in the fertile land between famous rivers of north India i.e. Ganga and Yamuna, known as *Doab*. It covers an area of 3747 Sq. Km. To the north the boundary of the district touches district Bulandshahar; on the northeast the Ganga separates it from the district Budaun; on the east and the south-east lies the district of Hathras; on the south-west lies the district of Mathura; and on the west it is separated from Haryana by the river Yamuna. (See Map-I, Annexure-1). The district is well connected with many cities and towns of the state and the country through famous historic Grand Trunk (G.T.) road or National Highway No.91 and broad gauge Delhi-Howrah railway line. New Delhi, national capital of India, is about 133 Kms. in its north whereas Lucknow, the capital of U.P., is about 400 Kms in its east.

Aligarh, headquarters city of the district, is known the world over for the famous seat of learning called Aligarh Muslim University, Aligarh and lock manufacturing industry. It was called *Kol* or *Koil* until 18th century. Mohammadgarh, Sabitgarh, Ramgarh, and Aligarh have been different names successively assigned to *Koil* at different times. The last three names were actually given to the Fort built about three miles to the north of the city which was a celebrated fortress of north India. The name Aligarh was conferred on it by Najaf Khan during the last quarter of the 18th century. The English after their occupation in 1803 extended the name of the Fort to the city itself (Siddiqui, 1975, Mann, 1992).

Textual historical references to the area, begin with the appearance of Muslim historians in 12th century AD, show *Koil* as important centre of administration, military and commerce. *Koil* first gained importance as Muslim military garrison and remained so throughout medieval period. It was made a *Shiqq* (District) by Sultans of Delhi and *sarkar* of Agra *suba* or province by Mughal emperors. Being both fertile and strategically important, and thanks to its proximity to Delhi, *Koil* was a valuable *zamindari* for Muslims, Marathas and British. Many famous Sultans and emperors of Delhi including Babur and Akbar and 14th century traveller Ibne Batuta visited *Koil* who described it as a handsome city of many gardens and mango trees. In the late eighteen century the region had witnessed rise of Jats who established their rules after defeating Rajputs. Many battles were fought among Jats, Najaf Khan, Afrasiyab Khan, Marathas etc. for the control of the region. Finally the British captured the fort of Aligarh on 4th September 1803 and formed the district of Aligarh in 1804 (Mann, 1992: 19-22).

The district has undergone various administrative changes since its formation. Presently it is divided into five *Tehsils* and 12 development blocks which are as follows:

Tehsil-wise Distribution of Blocks

Name of Tehsil	*Name of Block*
Koil	Lodha, Jawan Akrabad and Dhanipur
Khair	Khair and Tappal
Gabhana	Chandaus, Jawan
Atrauli	Atrauli, Bijoli and Gangiri
Iglas	Iglas and Gonda

The District is comprised of 1180 inhabited villages and 12 urban agglomerations namely Aligarh city (Municipal Corporation), Atrauli and Khair (Municipal Boards), Beswan, Iglas, Vijaygarh, Pilakhna, Kauriaganj, Jalali, Harduaganj,

Charra, and Jattari (town areas). Aligarh City is a part of *Tehsil Koil* which contains nearly half of the population of the district. (See Map II, Annexure-2).

Census of India 2001 enumerates 2992286 population of district Aligarh. More than two-third population of the district i.e. 71.10% (2127590) reside in villages and remaining lives in urban areas. Aligarh lags behind National Average on many indicators of human development. Sex-ratio (number of females per 1000 males) is 862 which is 71 points below to National Average i.e. 933. Average literacy rate is 58%, 7 points less than National Average. A whopping gap of 30 points exists between average literacy of males (71.10%) and females (43.30%) in the district. Work Participation Rate (WPR) is 30 points in the district, 9 points behind to National Average.

Agriculture is the mainstay of the economy despite the existence and expansion of small scale industrial units in the district. Locks, hardware, brassware are the main industries of the district. Aligarh is known the world over for manufacturing of different types of locks used in building doors, automobiles, suitcases, wooden and steel furniture etc. It is also known as "*Tala Nagiri*" (City of Locks). Recently manufacturing of glass beads has emerged as an important craft in the district. Manufacturing units of lock and other industrial artefacts are mostly located in urban areas, mainly in Aligarh city and provide employment to only 7% workers as per Census of India 2001. Remaining are agricultural workers (20%), Cultivators (32%) and other workers (41%) in the district as per Census of India 2001. The last category of workers is deceptive as it includes white-collar occupations on the one hand and blue-collar workers like rickshaw pullers and construction site workers, daily wage earners on the other. Maximum percentage of other workers (41%) is because of the fact that large number of people are daily wage earners in unorganized sector of economy in the district.

Muslims of District Aligarh

There are 6 major religious communities in the district whose population is as follows: Hindus- 2438496 (81.49%), Muslims-

Table 1

Population of Religious Communities, their Rural–Urban Distribution and Sex Ratio in the District

	Total	Male	%	Female	%	Sex Ratio	Rural Total	Rural Male	Rural %	Rural Female	Rural %	Urban Total	Urban Male	Urban %	Urban Female	Urban %
Community	2992286	1607402	53.72	1384884	46.28	862	2127592	1146456	53.89	981136	46.11	864694	460946	53.31	403748	46.69
Hindu	2438496	1313359	53.86	1125137	46.14	857	1913929	1033198	53.98	80731	46.02	524567	280161	53.41	244406	46.59
Muslim	531956	282449	53.10	249507	46.90	883	203710	107882	52.96	95828	47.04	328246	174567	53.18	153679	46.82
Christian	4187	2135	50.99	2052	49.01	961	1189	616	51.81	573	48.19	2998	1519	50.67	1479	49.33
Sikh	8145	4367	53.62	3778	46.38	865	3774	2072	54.90	1702	45.10	4371	2295	52.51	2076	47.49
Buddists	5093	2766	54.31	2327	45.69	841	3945	2121	53.76	1824	46.24	1148	645	56.18	503	43.82
Jain	3357	1749	52.10	1608	47.90	919	277	146	52.71	131	47.29	3080	1603	52.05	1477	47.95
Others	34	15	44.12	19	55.88	1267	3	0	0.00	3	100.00	31	15	48.39	16	51.61
Religion not stated	1018	562	55.21	456	44.79	811	765	421	55.03	344	44.97	253	141	55.73	112	44.27

Source: Uttar Pradesh Census of India 2001, "Report on Religion Data", Series 10, 2005

531956 (18%), Christians- 4187 (0.14%), Sikhs- 8145 (0.27%), Buddhists – 593 (0.17%), Jains- 3357 (0.11%), Others-34 (0.001%) and religion not stated- 1018 (0.03%). Population of religious communities, their rural–urban distribution and sex ratio in the district is presented in the Table No. 1.

Muslims appear highly urbanized community of the district as nearly sixty-two percent of them concentrate in urban areas. Hence their rate of urbanization is 32 percentage points more than the district average. Sex ratio among them is 883, 21 points more than the district average but 50 points less than the National Average. However, they are most illiterate community. Their literacy rate is only 45 per cent, 13 percentage points below to district average. Although a gap of 19 percentage points exists between literacy rate of Muslim male (54%) and female (35%), the gap is 11 percentage points less than district average. Similarly, their WPR is 26.38%, 4 points below to district average. Highest percentage (65.3%) of total Muslim workers (140343) in the district is of other workers which is followed by agricultural workers (15.6%), cultivators (11.1%) and household industry workers (8%). These figures are contrary to commonly held belief that most of the Muslim are household industry workers. Indeed, data show that Muslims are either dependent on agricultural sectors or engaged in menial occupations like rickshaw pulling, cycle repairing and many other low paid occupations in the informal sectors. Therefore, the highest percentage of Muslim workers is in the category of 'Other Workers'.

Muslims are not homogenous community. They are divided into hierarchically placed status groups called *baradaries*. Census of India 1931, the last Census which provides caste-wise information enumerated 35 *baradaries* of Muslims in the district (See Chapter-III). Few of these *baradaries* have higher social status while many of them are of lower social status. *Baradaries* of higher social status are called *Ashraf* who trace their origin from outside the country and Hindu higher castes converts. They had been military men, administrators, zamindars, and scholars until the independence of the country.

However, many of *Ashraf* families torn apart due to migration to Pakistan, and abolition of zamindari and, therefore, experienced rapid fall in their socio-economic status in post independent India. *Baradaries* of lower social status called *Ajlaf* have traditionally been landless and powerless communities, associated with service providing and menial occupations.

Methodology

A survey of 2500 Muslim households of selected villages and wards of towns of *Tehsil Koil* was conducted in May-June 2007 to examine their socio-economic and educational condition. *Tehsil Koil*, the largest *Tehsil* of district Aligarh was identified as a minority concentrated area by Ministry of Social Welfare and Justice, Government of India in 1993 for the implementation of Area Intensive and Madrasa Modernization Programme- the two mega schemes, clubbed into one scheme in Tenth Five Year Plan, launched by Govt. of India for educational uplift of minorities mainly Muslims. Attempt is being made in this report to present *Baradari*-wise socio-economic and educational status of Muslims. Furthermore, a survey of 89 schools located in surveyed localities was also conducted in order to assess the access of Muslims to these schools and their quality of education.

Census of India does not provide religion-wise population of villages and wards of urban localities. Therefore, we have purposively selected nine Muslim concentrated villages and twelve *mohallas* of three urban agglomeration namely Jalali, Pilakhna and Aligarh city. Since 61 per cent population of Muslims in district Aligarh concentrates in urban areas and remaining resides in villages, a sample of 1000 households from villages and remaining 1500 households from urban localities, in the ratio 40:60, is selected for the study. Technique of random sampling is used to identify households from different surveyed localities.

Block-wise distribution of villages and number of samples drawn from them is presented in Table No. 2 given below.

Table 2
Block wise Distribution of Sampled Villages and Households

Block	*Village*	*No. of Households*
Akrabad	Akrabad	153
	Mirza Chandpur	150
	Nanau	80
	Nanau (Nagla Rasaldar)	20
Dhanipur	Adhon	107
	Julupur Sihor (Faridpur)	92
Lodha	Ilyaspur	130
	Nagla Baraula	150
	Talaspur Khurd	118
	Total	1000

Mohalla-wise distribution of sampled households from three urban agglomerations is presented in the following Table No. 3.

Table 3
Urban Locality-wise Distribution of Sampled Mohallas and Households

Urban Locality	*Mohalla*	*No. of Households*
Aligarh City	Bhamola	123
	Bhujpura	175
	Jamalpur	173
	Jeevangarh	125
	M.A. Nagar	133
	Shahjamal	127
	Upper Fort	180
Jalali	Ameer	152
	Mehendi Ali	17
	Nagla Ausaf Ali	46
Pilakhana	Ansariyan	124
	Pathanan	125
	Total	1500

Aligarh City

Muslims constitute about 40 per cent population of Aligarh Municipal Corporation which was enumerated 669,087 by Census of India 2001. The city has grown rapidly in last two decades due to expansion of trade and commerce, educational institutions, emergence of Small Scale Industries, migration of people from villages to the city and so on. "The city was typically a *Qasbah* town scattered throughout North India. The town had local markets and acted as a regional centre of commercial and political activity. Its population of Hindus and Muslims, though distinct, displayed a great deal of homogeneity in social, political, and economic life, as well as much religious syncretism. Tombs of holy men (*pirs*) formed a moral centre for the town and their death anniversaries (*Urs*) were celebrated by both Hindus and Muslims alike. In Aligarh, there are two tombs (*Dargahs*), of Shah Jamal and Pir Bahadur, now known as Baba Barchi Bahadur" (Mann 1992: 23). "The apparently greater homogeneity in everyday life between Hindus and Muslims and in the political and economic life of the district contrasts dramatically with the subsequent polarization of identities during the British colonial period" (Ibid: 24). Slowly and gradually Aligarh has become a communally divided city due to various socio-economic and political factors emerged during freedom struggle and in post independent India.

Aligarh city is broadly divided into two parts i.e. Old City and Civil Lines area. The dividing line between the two part is railway line. Today both parts of the city have grown enormously due to emergence of satellite localities. The division of the town into two parts is not merely physical but also social and economic. Civil line is in the east of the railway line which was initially the area of government offices, AMU campus, and residences of Hindu and Muslim *zamindars* and wealthier businessmen. Many English medium schools, commercial centres, colonies of Hindu and Muslim middle class and slums dwellers have recently grown around civil line area. There is a dividing line between the residence of Hindus and Muslims in this part of the city.

The Old City is in the west of the railway line and has also, like civil line, grown enormously in recent years. Many satellite localities mostly slums have grown up around the old city. The old city's central point is Jama Masjid, located at the highest elevation in the area (Upper Kot). Nearby is the shrine of Shah Jamal, while the newer shrine of Baba Barchi is adjacent to the railway line. Close to Shah Jamal are the old and new

Idgahs where Muslim gather at the Eid festival. Hindu and Muslim mohallas are separated by narrow lanes and some mohallas have mixed population. All mohallas contain shops, factories and residences, but retail and wholesale outlets are concentrated on main roads leading in and out of the city. Density of population is very high whereas lanes and bye lanes are narrow in this part of the city whereby transportation is very difficult. There is acute problem of water logging during rainy season, sewer line which is a source of many unhygienic condition and disease. "Aligarhians say the town is characterized by four things, *makkhi, machchar, tale, nale* : flies, mosquitoes, locks and drains" (Mann). This part of the city houses two very old government degree colleges namely Dharam Samaj Degree College and Varshney Degree College, ITI, many Government Intermediate colleges and recently established English medium school on Aligarh-Agra road, Aligarh Mathura Road and Aligarh-Delhi road. All these educational institutions and other infrastructural facilities are mostly located in non-Muslim dominated localities. Muslims are compacted in densely populated mohallas and slums which are devoid of quality educational institutions and other government institutions.

As mentioned above 7 Muslim concentration localities of Aligarh City are selected for the survey (See Map–I). Three of these localities namely Upper Kot, Shah Jamal and Bhojpura are located in Old City whereas Jeevangarh, Bhamola, Jamalpur and M.A. Nagar are located in the east of the railway line but none of them has civic condition of Civil Lines. Located at the elevated site of the city, Upper Kot is a historical locality which, indeed, represent Muslim culture and society of Old City. Adjacent to Upper Kot are densely Muslim populated Shah Jamal and Bhojpura. Jeevangarh is located between Sir Syed Nagar (which houses residence of AMU teachers and other Muslim elite) and Ramghat Road. It is densely populated Muslim slum. Located adjacent to Shamshad Market, Bhamola has a sizeable population of University employees of low rank. Towards a kilometre south of Shamshad Market, Jamalpur is located between Anoopshahar Road and University boundary.

It is also a densely populated locality, mostly of poor and lower middle class Muslims. About a kilometre in south-west from Jamalpur is M.A. Nagar (Maulana Azad Nagar) which is a newly emerged peripheral Muslim locality. Most of the residents are migrated from villages of the district mainly after 1990 due to occurrence of communal violence.

Jalali is a Nagar Panchayat (town area), located at a distance of 20 kilometre in the east from Aligarh. It is connected with Grand Trunk Road with a metalled road which leads to Kasganj (presently district headquarters of district Kashi Ram Nagar). It is one of the oldest inhabited cites in the district. It was founded by Jalaluddin Khilji during the reign of Ghyasuddin Balban. The town had been an important military garrison during medieval time. Many of its inhabitants were renowned Syeds of Shia sect who migrated to different places in post independent India. It is still a Muslim concentration town of the district. Pilakhna is also a Muslim concentration Nagar Panchayat (town area), located at a distance of 6 kilometre in the east from the town Jalali. Meos (a backward Muslim *baradari*) are main inhabitant of the town who are mainly dependent upon agriculture and related occupations. Location of these towns and surveyed villages (which are mainly inhabited by Muslims) are shown in Map–II.

2

Population and Household Amenities

This chapter presents data, related with

(a) Demographic characteristics of surveyed households such as household size, sex-ratio, age composition and

(b) Nature of households and the basic amenities available to them.

Household Size

A survey of 1000 households of 9 selected villages, mentioned in preceding chapter, was conducted. Village-wise number of sample households, their size and population are presented in the following Table No. 1.

Household size among villagers is not uniform as shown in the above Table No. 1. It differs from one village to another. Highest household size, consisting of 8.25 persons exists in village Nanau (Nagla Rasaldar) whereas smallest size of 6.53 persons is in village Nagla Baraula. Average size of sample households is 7.43 persons, 1 point bigger than average household size of district Aligarh.

Size of household decreases in urban areas where the biggest household size is 7.52 and the smallest is 5.71. Fifteen hundred households of urban area contain 10047 persons and thus the average household size is 6.7, nearly equal to average household size of the district. This is shown in the following Table No. 2

Table 1
Household Size in Villages

Village Name	*No. of Households*	*Population*	*Average Size of Household*
Akrabad	153	1186	7.75
Mirza Chandpur	150	1177	7.85
Nanau	80	604	7.55
Nanau (Nagla Rasaldar)	20	165	8.25
Adhon	107	807	7.54
Julupur Sihor (Faridpur)	92	632	6.87
Ilyaspur	130	1016	7.82
Nagla Baraula	150	979	6.53
Talaspur Khurd	118	868	7.36
Total	1000	7434	7.43

Table 2
Household Size in Towns

Mohalla	*No. of Households*	*Population*	*Average Size of Household*
Bhamola	123	738	6
Bhujpura	175	1149	6.57
Jamalpur	173	1016	5.87
Jeevangarh	125	839	6.71
M.A. Nagar	133	966	7.26
Shahjamal	127	850	6.69
Upper Fort	180	1161	6.45
Ameer	152	1097	7.22
Mehendi Ali	17	97	5.71
Nagla Ausaf Ali	46	294	6.39
Ansariyan	124	932	7.52
Pathanan	125	908	7.26
Total	1500	10047	6.70

Two thousand five hundred sample households contain a population of 17481 and therefore average household size is 7.0, one point bigger than district average.

Age-Sex Composition of Population

Population of sampled households is classified into 5 age groups, presented in the following Table No. 3.

Table 3
Age Groups, Gender and Sex-Ratio

Age Groups	*Male*	*Female*	*Total*	*%*	*Sex Ratio*
0-6 Years	1680	1635	3315	18.96	973
7-14 Years	2159	2020	4179	23.91	936
15-35 Years	3478	3130	6608	37.80	900
36-60 Years	1498	1354	2852	16.31	904
Above 60 Years	264	263	527	3.01	996
Total	9079	8402	17481	100	925

Highest population 6608, as shown in the above Table No. 3, is found in the age group 15-35 years followed by population in the age group 7-14 years (4179), 0-6 years (3315), 36-60 years (2852) and above 60 years (527). Indeed, the first three age groups i.e. 0-6, 7-14 and 15-35 years constitute 80.67% population of sampled households. Hence the population of Muslims in *Tehsil Koil* may be described as young and productive. Lowest population in the age group 60 and above explicitly shows high mortality rate among Muslims in old age.

Sex-ratio, a critical demographic indicator, affecting status of females in India, is 925 as males outnumber females by 677 in a total population of 17481. This sex-ratio is higher than the average sex ratio of the district in 2001 by 63 points, and to the average sex ratio of Muslims in the district by 43 points. However, it is below to average sex-ratio of the country by 8 points.

Nevertheless, sex-ratio is not uniform in all age groups. It differs from one age group to another. Highest sex-ratio (996) is found in the age group 60 and above, followed by 0-6 age group (973). Sex-ratio in the age group 0-6 is called 'Child Sex-ratio' in Census operation which has become a serious socio-demographic problem of India due to its consistent declining rate during the last five decades. "It has declined from 976 in 1961 to 964 in 1971, 962 in 1981, 953 in 1991, and 927 in 2001. The low and falling child sex ratio is the result of two factors: excess female infant mortality (relative to male infant mortality) and female foeticide. Both in turn reflect parental discrimination against girls" (GoI, 2006: 33). Hence 973 child sex-ratio is obviously positive characteristic of sampled population. Indeed, Muslims of India "have highest child sex-ratio of any social group in the country as per the data of National Family Health Survey (NFHS)" GoI, 2006: 34).

Place of Origin and Migration

Migration of people from one place to another is an important demographic indicator which is caused by multiple socio-economic factors. Unemployment and lack of education, health and other civic amenities generally push people to migrate to those areas which promise them rather more opportunities of livelihood. Insecurity to life and property has emerged another important factor of migration, mainly for Muslims, due to frequent occurrence of communal violence in the last two and a half decade. Data about place of origin of household are collected to know the extent of in-migration and its causes in *Tehsil Koil*. Following Table 4 exhibits place of origin of household across rural-urban areas.

Table 4
Household's Place of Origin

	Rural		*Urban*		
Place of Origin	*No.*	*%*	*No.*	*%*	*Total*
Original Inhabitant of locality	790	79	1032	68.8	1822
Migrated from other village/town of Aligarh	114	11.4	255	17	369
Outside Aligarh but within UP	93	9.3	180	12	273
Outside U.P.	3	0.3	33	2.2	36
Total	1000	40	1500	60	2500

The above table reveals that out of 2500 households 1822 (78.8%) are original inhabitant of sampled localities. Remaining 678 (27.12%) migrated to sample villages and *mohallas* from other places.

More than half of the migrated households i.e. 369 (54.52%) are from district Aligarh whereas 273 (40.26%) households come to reside in sampled villages and *mohallas* from other districts of Uttar Pradesh. Only 36 households migrated from outside Uttar Pradesh.

It is commonly believed that people migrate from villages to towns and cities. This is contradicted by the data of this study which show that 210 (21%) out of 1000 village households are migrated. However, the percentage of migrated households in urban areas is 10 percentage points more than villages i.e. 468 (31.2%).

Reasons of Migration are tabulated and presented in the table given below

Largest number of households 452 out of 678, as evident from the Table No. 5, migrated for employment. Problem of insecurity to life and property is reported to have been the cause of migration by 85 households. It is appropriate here to note that frequent occurrence of Hindu-Muslim violence in both rural and urban areas in district Aligarh in the last two and half decade accelerated insecurity among Muslims which compel them for migration to Muslim concentration villages and *mohallas*.

Another factor of migration is related with the problem of social insecurity. Therefore, 77 households migrated to live near their relatives so they may have support of their relatives during the time of life crisis and emergent situation. To avail educational opportunity is yet another reason of migration for 57 households. Besides, there are other reasons of migration such as dispute in family, death of husband, cost of land etc.

Household Types

Surveyed households are classified on the basis of their composition, headship and type of habitation.

Simple and Complex Households

Households are classified into simple and complex. A simple household is composed of husband and wife (or any one of them) and their unmarried children. It also includes a conjugal household which does not have any child at the time of survey due to reasons such as just married, physical deformity and death of children. On the contrary, a complex household comprises of more than one simple household. For example a household of husband-wife with their married children or a

Table 5
Causes of In-migration

	Rural-Urban Categories				
	Rural		*Urban*		
Reasons for Migration	*No.*	*%*	*No.*	*%*	*Total*
Security	28	32.94	57	67.06	85
Education	12	21.05	45	78.95	57
Employment	128	28.32	324	71.68	452
Relatives	40	51.95	37	48.05	77
Dispute in the family	1	50.00	1	50.00	2
Due to death of husband shifted to her maternal Village	0	0.00	1	100.00	1
Due to low rate of land	0	0.00	2	100.00	2
House was damaged	0	0.00	1	100.00	1
Marriage	1	100.00	0	0.00	1
Total	210	30.97	468	69.03	678

household of two or more married brothers in the absence of parents. Common residence is used as another criterion for defining a complex household.

Survey data reveal 1650 simple and remaining complex households. Hence only 34 per cent households are found to be complex. Percentage of complex households is 40 in villages whereas it is 29 per cent in urban areas. Distribution of simple and complex households in villages and towns is presented in Table No. 6. given below.

Table 6
Rural-Urban Distribution of Simple and Complex Household

	No. of Household				
	Rural		*Urban*		
Nature of Household	*No.*	*%*	*No.*	*%*	*Total*
Simple	598	59.8	1052	70.13	1650
Complex	402	40.2	448	29.87	850
Total	1000	40	1500	60	2500

Male-Female Headed Households

Surveyed households are found to be both male and female headed. It is being observed that there are three types of female headed households in the universe of the study which are as follows:

(a) Husband does not earn for the livelihood of his wife and children due to his physical handicap or bad habits. It is the wife who earns for her husband and children and she is being declared head of the household by her husband.

(b) An aged widow considered head of the household by her children.

(c) A young widow with her dependent children.

Male female headed households in both rural and urban areas are presented in the following Table 7 which exhibits that there are 245 (9.8%) female headed households. Percentage of female headed households is more in urban areas i.e.10% than in villages 9.5%

Table 7
Rural–Urban Distribution of Male and Female Headed Households

	No. of Households				
	Male Headed		*Female Headed*		
Categories (Area Type)	*No.*	*%*	*No.*	*%*	*Total*
Rural	905	90.5	95	9.5	1000
Urban	1350	90	150	10	1500
Total	2255	90.2	245	9.8	2500

Type of Habitation

Type of habitation is a significant criterion for the classification of households. Indeed, the type of habitation exhibits socio-economic condition of households. Surveyed households are classified into four categories i.e. *Pucca, Kuchcha, Mixed and Jhopri.* A *Pucca* house is one which is constructed with cement, brick and concrete whereas, a *Kuchcha* house is made of clay. Mixed house contains construction of cement and concrete as well as clay and *Jhopri* is a makeshift house made with bamboo, grass and tarpaulin. Type of habitation across rural–urban is presented in the following Table 8.

Table 8
Type of Habitation Across Rural-Urban Categories

	No. of Households				
Habitation Type	*Rural*	*Percent*	*Urban*	*Percent*	*Total*
Kuchcha	198	19.80	195	13.00	393
Pucca	366	36.60	878	58.53	1244
Mixed	358	35.80	373	24.87	731
Jhopri	78	7.80	54	3.60	132
Total	1000	100.00	1500	100.00	2500

Nearly half of the surveyed households, as shown in the above Table No. 8 have *pucca* residence whereas 29.24% live in residence of 'mixed' category. Remaining 21% reside in either '*Kuchcha*' house or in '*Jhopri*' categories of habitation.

A wide gap is found between villages and towns in regard to condition of habitation. Village households appear to be more deprived than households of towns. For only 36.60% households of villages as against 58.53% in towns possess *pucca* residence. Percentage of remaining habitation type in villages is more than urban areas. For instance 19.80% village households as against 13.00% in urban areas reside in *'Kuchcha'* habitation. Similarly, percentage of habitation of 'Mixed' and "*Jhopri'* categories is 35.80% and 7.80% respectively which is higher to 24.87% and 3.60% in urban areas.

Basic Household Amenities

Drinking Water

All surveyed households of both rural and urban areas do not have facility of drinking water within the premises of the residence. About 40 per cent households of villages are deprived of drinking water facility within their premise. For 610 out of 1000 village households are found to have facility of drinking water within their homes. The source of water for them is handpumps which generally do not effectively work during summer days due to declining water level. Therefore, they face enormous difficulties for fetching safe drinking water in the season of summer. Those 40 per cent households who do not have facility of drinking water within their homes are dependent upon government installed hand pumps in villages.

On the contrary, about 82 per cent (1233) households of urban areas have drinking water facility within their premises. Thus 18 per cent households in urban areas are deprived of drinking water facilities in their houses. Most of the households in which drinking facility is available fetch water from hand pumps. Very few have the facility of tap water or submersible pump. Problem of safe drinking water in urban areas is acute for those who do not have the facility in their houses because government hand pumps are neither adequately available nor properly managed. Therefore, people of urban areas have to walk a considerable distance for fetching the water. Water contamination and decline in its level compounds the problem of safe drinking water for urban households.

Electricity

Electricity too is not available to all surveyed households. Only 319 (32%) households of villages have electricity. Therefore, 68 per cent rural households are deprived of an important basic household amenity. The position of urban households is comparatively better but not rosy. For 521 out of 1500 (35%) urban households are deprived of electricity. Electricity is an acute problem in all areas of Uttar Pradesh due to its erratic and insufficient supply, *Tehsil Koil* is not an exception.

Sanitation

Toilet facility is also not available to all households of villages despite govt. of India's scheme called Total Sanitation Campaign (TSA) whereby aid is provided to Below Poverty Line (BPL) households for construction of toilets. Only 340 out of 1000 (34%) households of villages are found having toilet facility within the premise of their residence. However, most of these toilets are dry latrines. Very few are leach pit and septic tank. Those who do not have toilet facility within their homes go to open field for defecation.

The condition of households in urban areas is comparatively better in regard to availability of toilet facility. For 1116 out of 1500 (74.4%) urban households have toilet facility within their homes. Most of these toilets are either leach pit or septic tank. In this way a considerable number (24.6%) of households in urban areas are still deprived of toilet facility. They go for defecation in polluted and unhygienic open areas.

Apart from the above-mentioned basic household amenities, surveyed households are also found to be deprived of other facilities such as bathroom, kitchen and verandah which are essential for hygienic, healthy and dignified living condition. Only 296 (29.6%) rural households as against 933 (62.2%) urban households have bathroom in their houses.

Separate kitchen is available to few households in both rural and urban areas. Only 179 (17.9%) rural households and 597 (39.8%) urban households possess separate kitchen. Most of these kitchens are small in size and unhygienic.

Domestic Gadgets and Vehicles

Ownership of domestic gadgets like refrigerator, television, radio, etc., and vehicles for transportation such as car and motorcycle is another indicator of household's living condition. Large number of surveyed households are found to be deprived of essential domestic appliances and vehicles for transportation which shows wide spread poverty among Muslims of *Tehsil Koil.* Data related with the possession of these gadgets and vehicles are presented in the Table No. 9 given below:

Table 9
Domestic Gadgets and Vehicles in Urban-Rural Households

	Sampled Households Across Availability of General Assets in the House				
Assets	*Rural*	*Rural %*	*Urban*	*Urban %*	*Total*
Refrigerator	75	17.2	361	82.8	436
Bicycle	423	32.94	861	67.06	1284
Motor cycle	85	26.48	236	73.52	321
Car	11	29.73	26	70.27	37
Radio	132	31.35	289	68.65	421
Tape recorder	48	25.81	138	74.19	186
T.V.	161	21.73	580	78.27	741
VCD	56	28	144	72	200
Landline Telephone	26	26	74	74	100
Mobile	142	26.59	392	73.41	534
Computer	6	12	44	88	50

Ration Card: Legally, every household must be listed in the record of village and town and issued a ration card by Government Agencies. Ration Card is an identity card of a household as well as a license for availing benefits of Government schemes including Public Distribution System (PDS). Hence a household may face serious problems in establishing its identity mainly before government agencies, if it does not possess ration card.

Government agencies conduct a survey to identify Above Poverty Line (APL) and Below Poverty Line (BPL) households and accordingly issue ration cards to them. Below Poverty Line households are classified into two categories i.e. simple and poorest. Ration card of yellow colour is issued to APL households whereas, ration card of red colour is for simple BPL households. White colour ration card is issued to poorest among poor.

The data of this study exhibit that 50 households (5%) of villages and 117 (8%) of urban areas do not possess ration card. Details about possession of ration card in both rural and urban areas is presented in the Table No. 10 given below:

Table 10
Possession of Ration Card Across Rural-Urban Areas

	Sampled Households Across Availability of Ration Card					
Ration Card	*Rural*	*Rural %*	*Urban*	*Urban %*	*Total*	*Total %*
None	50	5.0	117	7.8	167	6.68
Yellow	865	86.5	1244	82.9	2109	84.36
White	61	6.1	105	7.0	166	6.64
Red	24	2.4	34	2.3	58	2.32

It is important to note here that about 9% households of rural and urban areas have been issued ration card of red and white colour despite the fact, as the data of this study show, poverty is rampant among surveyed households. More than 50% surveyed household are deprived of basic amenities.

3

Baradaries and Administrative Classification

Unlike popular perception, Muslims are not homogenous community. They are internally divided into various *Baradaries* (caste-like hierarchical status groups) and classes (economic groups). This chapter presents Muslim *Baradaries* of district Aligarh, recorded by Census of India 1931 (the last caste-wise Census of India) as well as *Baradaries* of surveyed households. Muslim *Baradaries* are administratively classified into General and Other Backward Classes (OBCs) by both Central and State Governments. Hence an attempt is made to explore the knowledge of Respondents about administrative status of their *Baradaries*.

Castes and *Baradaries*

Caste system is organically linked institution of Indian society, existing since time immemorial. Having its origin in *Verna scheme* (All India cultural model of classifying Hindus into four social groups i.e. *Brahmans, Kshtriyas, Vaishyas,* and *Sudras*) and legitimized by Hindu doctrines of *karma, dharma,* rebirth, purity, pollution and so on, the caste system has evolved over a period of time as a complex, rigid and closed system of stratification. Being a 'Unique Institution' of wider social ramifications, it has been fascinating scholars of both India and abroad for a long period of time and, therefore, innumerable studies about multiple dimensions of caste system have been made. Sociologists and social anthropologists have studied caste system with different theoretical perspectives such as functional, structural, Marxists, and so on and, therefore, various explanations about caste system are available. However, almost all sociologists and social anthropologists observe caste system as a micro structure, consisting of hundreds of regional endogamous groups. Some of the major features of the systems are as follows:

(a) *Hereditary*- Membership of caste is ascriptive and not achieved. However mobility from one caste to another, mainly from lower to higher caste through the process of *sanskritization*, and consequently adoption of higher caste name have been recorded by scholars which is not theoretically permissible.

(b) *Hierarchy*- Ordering castes higher and lower with one another on the scale of social status. Everywhere in India Brahmins are at the top and *Shudras* are at the bottom in the caste hierarchy. Between these two polar opposite positions other castes have different status in caste hierarchy of different regions.

(c) *Endogamy*- The most enduring feature of the caste system which enjoins a person to marry within his/her caste

(d) *Association with an Occupation*- Occupations are hierarchically classified and, therefore, are normatively assigned to different castes according to their social status. Empirical evidences, however, exhibit that castes entered into the terrain of other caste's occupations except those of Brahmins and untouchables.

(e) *Purity and Pollution*- A cultural and ideological characteristic, permanently divides castes into pure and polluted. This is originator of social distancing and untouchability practice which differs from region to region.

Thus, caste system has both cultural features such as hierarchy, purity and pollution, and doctrine of *karma* and *dharma* and structural features like institutionalized inequalities of status and power and restriction on marriage, occupation, inter-dining and social relationships. Structural features, if not cultural features, of caste system are also found among followers of those religions which are principally against institutionalized system of inequalities. Hence caste system is an all India institution, existing across religious communities.

Baradaries, like castes, are hereditary and hierarchical endogamous groups, having traditional association with distinctive occupations. They are, indeed, status groups, a major source of internal social distinction and unequal distribution of social status and power among Muslims. E. A. Mann in her study of Muslims of Aligarh city writes, "A word of Persian origin literally meaning 'brotherhood', a Baradari possesses an internalised sense of solidarity extended to its members, but denied to those outside its limit. It is imbued with a sense of honour *(izzat)*, on the basis of which it is ranked higher or lower in relation to other *Baradaries*. Its meaning, therefore, largely conforms to Weber's description of a status group... The term has currency not only among Muslims of west UP, but also among Hindus, and has been used interchangeably by both scholars of Hindu and Muslim society," (1992 : 44).

Zat is another word which is frequently used interchangeably with the word *Baradari*. However, it has wider and diffused meaning; indeed a status category rather than a status group. "It normally refers to the higher status categories of Saiyyid, Sheikh, Pathan and Mughal. Within the *zat* are also *Baradaries*, endogamous sub-units of the wider unit, whose principal criterion of membership is marriage" (Ibid: 47).

> "In Aligarh, the meaning of Baradari is understood to be a named, endogamous status group associated with a specific occupation are lineage, from which it often, but not always, derives its name. Nowadays the correlation between occupation and Baradari is not as systematic as in the past, but ancestral occupation perceives the individual when defining status in relation to other Muslims, and hence in relation to marriage and work prospects... while the internal structure of a Baradari is regulated by marriage, external boundaries consolidated by residential locality, by an ascribed social identity, by restrictions on social intercourse and commensality, and by strongly held beliefs that certain forms of behaviour are associated with Baradari identity" (Ibid: 44-53).

Thus, *Baradaries* have almost all structural characteristics of Hindu caste system. This has been, much before the work of E.A. Mann, noted and explained by Ghaus Ansari (1960), Imtiaz Ahmad (1973) and other sociological studies on Muslims social structure. Reports of Government Committees such as PHLC (2006) and National Commission on Religious and Linguistic Minorities (NCRLM 2007) also recognized presence of castes or descent based social stratification among Muslims.

PHLC reports that:

> "The Census of India, 1901 listed 133 social groups wholly or partially Muslim. The present day Muslim Society in India is divided into four major groups: (i) the Ashrafs who trace their origins to foreign lands such as Arabia, Persia, Turkistan or Afghanistan, (ii) the upper caste Hindus who converted to Islam, (iii) the middle caste converts whose occupations are ritually clean, (iv) the converts from the erstwhile untouchable castes, Bhangi (scavenger), Mehtar (sweeper), Chamar (tanner), Dom and so on.
>
> These four groups are usually placed into two broad categories, namely, 'ashraf' and 'ajlaf'. The former, meaning noble, includes all Muslims of foreign blood and converts from higher castes. While 'ajlaf' meaning degraded or unholy, embraces the ritually clean occupational groups and low ranking converts. In Bihar, U.P and Bengal, Sayyads, Sheikhs, Moghuls and Pathans constitute the 'ashrafs'. The 'ajlaf', are carpenters, artisans, painters, graziers, tanners, milkmen etc. According to the Census of 1901, the ajlaf category includes 'the various classes of converts who are known as Neo Muslim in Bihar and Nasya in North Bengal. It also includes various functional groups such as that of the Jolaha or weaver, Dhunia or cotton-carder, Kulu or oil-presser, Kunjra or vegetable-seller, Hajjam or barber, Darzi or tailor, and the like.' The 1901 Census also recorded the presence of a third category called Arzal: 'It consists of the very lowest castes, such as the Halalkhor, Lalbegi, Abdal, and Bediya...'. Similar Pattern of descent based social stratification is discernible in other regions (*like Kerala, Andhra Pradesh*) as well" (2006: 192-193, italics added).

Sociologically, thus Muslims are divided into three broad categories i.e. '*Ashraf*', '*Ajlaf*' and '*Arzal*'. However, administratively they are classified into two categories i.e. General and OBCs.

For *Arzals* have been excluded from Scheduled Caste (SC) category (initially composed of Hindu untouchable castes and later on castes of Sikhs and Buddhists were added) by Presidential Order (1950) and, therefore, bracketed with the *Ajlaf*. It is the *Ajlaf* and *Arzal* who generally constitute Muslim OBCs. "Thus, the OBCs among Muslims constitute two broad categories. The halalkhors, helas, lalbegis or bhangis (scavengers), dhobis (washermen), nais or hajjams (barbers), chiks (butchers), faqirs (beggars) etc belonging to the 'Arzals' are the 'untouchable converts' to Islam that have found their way in the OBC list. The *momins* or *julahas* (weavers), *darzi* or *idrisis* (tailors), *rayeens* or *kunjaras* (vegetable sellers) are Ajlafs or converts from 'clean' occupational castes." (Ibid: 193).

Muslim *Baradaries* of District Aligarh

Decennial Census in post-independent India (from 1951 onwards) discontinued practice of recording castes/*baradaries*. The last Census, provided caste-wise data, was conducted in 1931. Muslim *baradaries* in district Aligarh, as per the data of 1931 Census, are presented in the Table No. 1 given below:

Table 1
Muslims Baradaries in Aligarh District in 1931

Male	Female	Total	Baradari
7	-	7	Ahir
39	46	85	Barhai
2	1	3	Bhangi
622	536	1158	Bharbhunja
50	28	78	Bhat
7661	6868	14529	Bahishti (*Bhishti*)
-	6	6	Chamar
76	58	134	Darzi
964	873	1837	Dhobi
100	74	174	Dhunia
35	44	79	Dome
7669	6854	14523	Fakir
8	-	8	Gadariya
778	667	1445	Gaddi
39	23	62	Halwai

Contd.

Male	Female	Total	Baradari
2281	1846	4127	Julaha
4	13	17	Kalwar
90	66	156	Kumhar
782	583	1365	Kunjra
2307	1895	4202	Lohar
1673	1209	2882	Manihar
22	16	38	Meo
507	350	857	Mughal
659	604	1263	Nai
88	83	171	Nat
1827	1686.	3513	Nau-Muslim
12011	9602	21613	Pathan
2733	2127	4860	Qassab
5505	4811	10316	Rajput
3833	2898	6731	Saiyyid
19360	15291	34651	Sheikh
8	8	16	Sonar
9	5	14	Tamboli
5923	4966	10889	Teli
3	3	6	Turk
6602	5567	12169	Others
251	231	482	Not specified
84528	69938	154466	Total

Source: Census of India, 1931, United Provinces of Agra and Oudh, Vol. XVIII, Part-II, By A.C. Turner (Allahabad; 1933), Quoted from E.A. Mann1992: 52

It is evident from the above table that 35 *baradaries* as well as categories of 'Others' and 'Not Specified' constituted about 1,54,466 population of district Aligarh in 1931. These *baradaries* belong to sociological categories of *'Ashraf'* such as Saiyyid, Mughal ,Pathan, etc., *'Ajlaf'* such as Julaha, Qassab, Dhunia etc., and *'Arzal'* such as Bhangi, Nat, Chamar, Dome etc. Having the population of 34,651 Sheikh was the largest *baradari* of *Ashraf* Category followed by Pathans (21,613)and Saiyyids (6,731) whereas Bhishtis, numbering 14,529, were the largest *baradari* of *Ajlaf* category followed by Fakir (14,523), Teli (1088). Highest proportion of Sheikhs and Pathans in Muslim population might be due to the process of *Ashrafization* or reporting title of Sheikh and Pathans to Census enumerators by lower castes. Indeed, reporting titles of higher castes by lower castes was a general trend, existing across religious communities in colonial India. Sheikhs and Pathans were the titles which were adopted by many households of *Ajlaf baradaries*. Pattern of mobility from a *baradari* of lower status to that of higher status reflected in a Persian proverb, widely quoted locally, meaning "Yesterday our work was butchery (Qassab), then we became Sheikhs; having acquired a taste for that, tomorrow if the harvest is good, we shall with the grace of God become Saiyyids".

If we classify above mentioned *baradaries* into present day administrative categories i.e. Muslim General and OBCs, we find Mughals, Pathans, Rajput, Saiyyids, Sheikhs and Turk as well as Others and Not Specified constituted 56 per cent population of Muslims and the remaining 44 per cent population was composed of *baradaries* listed in the administrative category of OBCs.

Baradaries of Surveyed Households

Responding to the question "What is the name of your caste/ baradari?", Respondents reported various names of their *baradaries*, many of which appeared to be names of *baradaries* of a *Zat*, recently adopted titles for claiming higher status and occupations. This response is presented in Column-II of the Table No. 2 given below. What is the real or original name of your *baradari* was the second question asked to them. Answer of this question was generally precise which is presented alphabetically in Column-I of the Table No. 2 on the following page.

Except 20 Respondents which are classified as 'Not Specified' in the above table all have reported names of their *baradari*. Six of 'Not Specified' category reported themselves as 'Muslims'. They argued Islam does not recognise *baradari* system while remaining 14 did not disclose their *baradari* name. They were poor migrants, living in *Jhopris* in Aligarh city. In this way 2480 households reported their 32 *baradaries* out of which 24 namely *Banjara, Bawarchi, Bhishti, Bhurji, Chunpat, Darzi, Dhobi, Dhuna, Fakir, Gaddi, Ghosi, Jhoja, Kumhar, Lohar, Mahigir, Manihar, Mewati, Momin Ansari, Nai, Qassab, Rangrez, Rayeen, Sangtarash,* and *Teli* figure either in both Central and

Table 2
Baradaries Surveyed Households

Castes	*Response of The Respondents*	*Rural*	*Urban*	*Total*
Banjara	Banjara Muslim	3	0	3
Bawarchi	Sheikh Bawarchi	0	1	1
Bhishti	Saqqe, Abbasi, Abbasi Khan, Sheikh Abbasi, Saqqe Bhishti, Panihare (Ajmeri Pathan)	112	265	377
Bhurji	Bharbhunja, Muniri, Bhurji Pathan	22	10	32
Chunpat	Chunpat, Chunnewale, Alvi Chunpati, Chipat	0	3	3
Darzi	Idrisi	1	8	9
Dhobi	Dhobi Qassar, Qasar, Qasa, Muslim Dhobi,	0	35	35
Dhuna	Mansoori, Naddaf	0	6	6
Fakir	Alvi Syed, Mian Saheb, Syed Fakir, Miyan Fakir, Saifi Fakir, Sheikh Abbasi (Fakir)	164	132	296
Farooqui	Farooqui	0	1	1
Gaddi	Ghazi, Gaddi	0	7	7
Ghosi	Dhodheye, Ghosi Pathan, Ghosi	1	6	7
Jhoja	Jhoja Pathan	0	18	18
Kumhar	Muslim Kumhar	3	0	3
Lohar	Saifi, Saifi Lohar, Khan Saifi	99	76	175
Mahigir	Fisherman, Machhliwale, Sheikh Mahigir	1	5	6
Manihar	Manihar Siddiqui, Churihar, Sheeshgar	89	41	130
Mewati	Meo, Mewati, Mewati Bhagolia	154	111	265
Momin Ansari	Ansari, Weaver, Julaha, Momin Ansar	3	102	105
Mughal	Mirza, Beg, Mughal Pathan, Pathan Mughal (kabuli)	16	14	30
Nai	Sulemani, Salmani, Hajjam	2	10	12
Pathan	Khan, Khan Siddiqi, Pathan Syed, Pathan Baraich, Khan Saheb, Afghani, Ghauri, Yusufzai, Ghauri Pathan, Bhoori Pathan, Khan Sherwani, Sherwani Pathan	17	248	265
Qassab	Qureshi, Bade Qasai, Sheikh Qureshi	12	119	131

Contd.

Castes	*Response of The Respondents*	*Rural*	*Urban*	*Total*
Rajput	Muslim Rajput, Adbharia, Chauhan, Jadon, Bargujar Thakur, Rathore Pathan, Yadav Thakur, Jadon Thakur, Chaudhari, Janhare, Pawar, Rajput Pathan, Tomar Neo-Muslims,Pundhir, Mirza Rajput, Mirza Jadon, Khan Rajput,	230	60	290
Rangrez	Rangrez	0	7	7
Rayeen	Sabzi Farosh, Kunjra	0	19	19
Sangtarash	Naqqashi or Naqqash	0	1	1
Shamshi	Shamshi	0	4	4
Sheikh	Sheikh Zuberi, Sheikh Faridi, Sheikh Shia, Sheikh Farooqui, Sheikh Siddiqui, Qureshi, Sheikh Pathan, Sheikh Syed,	6	76	82
Syed	Syed Shia, Syed Sunni, Syed Naqvi, Syed Zaidi, Syed Qazi,Syed Jafari, Arabi Syed, Syed Baghdadi, Israili Syed, Shamshi Syed	5	48	53
Teli	Malik, Rogangar, Rogan Malik, Usmani, Shahbani	59	47	106
Warsi	Warsi	0	1	1
Not Specified		1	19	20
Total		1000	1500	2500

State Lists of OBCs or any one of them. Hence remaining 8 *baradaries* belong to the category of General. In this way 1758 (70.32%) of surveyed households belong to the category of OBCs.

Awareness About Administrative Status of *Baradaries*

In keeping with the diversities of the people and different causes for backwardness, three distinct groups were recognized in the Constitution for making special provisions for their advancement. These were (1) Scheduled Castes, (2) Scheduled Tribes and (3) Socially and educationally backward classes or Other Backward Classes (OBCs). The first group is religion specific as it includes only castes of Hindus, Buddhists and Sikhs. Whereas the last two groups are all inclusive and do not discriminate on the basis of religion. They include castes/communities of every religious group. Constitution of India provides various safeguards and affirmative action to SC and ST and accordingly series of programmes and schemes were launched for their welfare by both Central and State governments. Muslims are deprived of benefits available to SCs and STs as (a) they do not figure in the group of SCs and (b) very few of their communities are included in STs, though many more Muslim communities deserve to be included in this category. Furthermore, Muslim STs are more illiterate and poor than non-Muslim STs. Therefore, they are unable to avail the benefits available to STs. The same is the case with Muslim *baradaries,* included in the group of Socially and educationally backward classes. They too are more illiterate, poor and unorganized than non-Muslim OBCs. Hence they are deprived of the benefits available to OBCs. It is reported by many scholars and Government committees that many of the excluded and deprived OBCs are not aware about the administrative status of their castes. For they are illiterate, poor as well as excluded from the benefits of schemes, launched for their welfare. Awareness is a pre-requisite to avail or struggle to avail benefits of Government schemes. Therefore, questions were asked to explore the awareness among Muslims about administrative status of their *baradaries.* This is presented in the Table No. 3 given below. Column-I of the Table indicates administrative status of *Baradaries* whereas Column-II mention the name of the *Baradaries* included in particular administrative category. Responses of the Respondents are presented in Column -III, IV and V.

Table 3
Awareness about Administrative Status of Baradaries

	Response of Respondent				
Category	*Baradaries*	*General*	*O.B.C.*	*Don't Know*	*Total*
General	1. Farooqui	0	1	0	1
General	2. Mughal	12	0	18	30
General	3. Pathan	149	9	107	265
General	4. Rajput	127	11	152	290
General	5. Shamshi	1	3	0	4
General	6. Sheikh	42	6	34	82
General	7. Syed	33	0	20	53
General	8. Warsi	0	0	1	1
OBC	9. Banjara	0	0	3	3
OBC	10. Bawarchi	0	0	1	1
OBC	11. Bhisti	26	87	264	377
OBC	12. Bhurji	4	6	22	32
OBC	13. Chunpat	0	0	3	3
OBC	14. Darzi	1	3	5	9
OBC	15. Dhobi	0	11	24	35
OBC	16. Dhuna	0	4	2	6
OBC	17. Fakir	13	81	202	296
OBC	18. Gaddi	1	4	2	7
OBC	19. Ghosi	0	1	6	7
OBC	20. Jhoja	2	8	8	18
OBC	21. Kumhar	0	0	3	3
OBC	22. Lohar	14	68	93	175
OBC	23. Mahigir	0	3	3	6
OBC	24. Manihar	13	30	87	130
OBC	25. Mewati	52	34	179	265
OBC	26. Momin Ansari	4	46	55	105
OBC	27. Nai	1	3	8	12
OBC	28. Qassab	28	27	76	131
OBC	29. Rangrez	0	4	3	7
OBC	30. Rayeen	0	6	13	19
OBC	31. Sangtarash	0	1	0	1
OBC	32. Teli	7	41	58	106
	33. Not Specified	0	0	20	20
	Total	530	498	1472	2500

Table No. 3. explicitly shows that 1472 (58.88%) Respondents do not know administrative status of *Baradaries* into General and OBCs. All 20 (100%) Respondents of Not Specified category, 1120 out of 1754 (63.85%) of OBC category and 332 out of 726 (45.73%) of General category do not have awareness about the administrative classification of *Baradaries*. Hence Respondents of General category are more aware than Respondents of OBC category about administrative classification of Castes/*Baradaries*.

One thousand twenty-eight (41.12%) Respondents reported the status of their *Baradari* either as General or OBC. All of them do not have exact awareness about the administrative status of their *Baradari*. For example 30 (4.13%) Respondents of General category reported themselves as OBCs whereas 166 (9.46%) Respondents of OBC category reported themselves as General. In this way 50 per cent Respondents of General category and 26.68 per cent of OBC have correct awareness about the administrative status of their *Baradari*.

4

Workers and Occupations

Work Participation Rate/Workers Population Ratio (WPR) provides an idea of the extent of participation in economic activity by the population. Ability to find work is a function of assets (both physical and others) and opportunities of work available. Nature of work/occupation decisively affects social and economic status of a worker. This chapter presents data about workers (their incomes and occupations), in the population of sampled households.

Worker Participation Rate

Surveyed households have a population of 17481. Out of which 3926 are reported to be workers. Hence WPR is 22 per cent. No significant difference of WPR exists between rural and urban areas. For there are 1623 workers in 7434 population (21.83%) of rural households whereas 10047 population of urban household contains 2303 workers (22.93%). A comparison between WPR of surveyed households and that of district average (including rural and urban) is given below:

	District Aligarh	*Surveyed Households*
Average	30.6	22
Urban	25.5	22.93
Rural	32.7	21.83

Thus, rural households appear to be much deprived of economic participation.

Workers and Income Groups

Respondents are asked to report monthly income of workers of their households. Their responses are tabulated into four income groups i.e. up to 2000, 2001-5000, 5001-10000 and more than 10,000 which is presented in the Table 1 given below:

Table 1
Worker's Income Groups

Categories	*Non-Workers*	*Up to 2000 (in Rs.)*	*2001-5000*	*5001-10000*	*>10000*	*Total*
	No.	*No.*	*No.*	*No.*	*No.*	*No.*
Rural	5811	1157	410	50	6	7434
Urban	7744	1333	770	153	47	10047
Total	13555	2490	1180	203	53	17481

Largest number of workers i.e. 2490 (63.42%), as shown in the above Table No. 1, are found of lowest income group. Number of workers sharply decline as the income group goes up. Thus 1180 workers (30.06%) belong to second income group, followed by 203 (5.17%) in the third income group and 53 (1.35%) in the highest income group.

Workers of rural households appear to be more poor than that of urban households. For 71.29 per cent rural workers as against 57.88 per cent urban workers belong to lowest income group. Their percentage in different income groups is as follows:

	Up to 2000 (in Rs.) Percent	*2001-5000 (in Rs.) Percent*	*5001-10000 (in Rs.) Percent*	*>10000 (in Rs.) Percent*
Rural	71.29	25.26	3.08	0.37
Urban	57.88	33.43	6.64	2.04

Workers' Income Groups Across *Baradaries*

Income groups of workers across their *Baradaries* are tabulated and presented in the following Table No. 2.

Table 2
Workers' Income Groups Across *Baradaries*

		Non-Workers	*Upto 2000*	*2001-5000*	*5001-10000*	*> 10000*	*Total*
Caste	*Categories*	*No.*	*No.*	*No.*	*No.*	*No.*	*No.*
Farooqui	General	1	1	0	0	0	2
Mughal	General	195	24	17	3	1	240
Pathan	General	1313	227	143	30	12	1725
Rajput	General	1683	297	99	31	8	2118
Shamshi	General	17	5	2	0	1	25
Sheikh	General	341	72	42	21	8	484
Syed	General	234	28	29	16	10	317
Warsi	General	3	0	2	0	0	5
Banjara	OBC	21	5	0	0	0	26
Bawarchi	OBC	7	0	1	0	0	8
Bhisti	OBC	1999	400	182	19	0	2600
Bhurji	OBC	173	52	2	1	0	228
Chunpat	OBC	13	2	1	0	0	16
Darzi	OBC	54	11	4	0	0	69
Dhobi	OBC	163	40	20	1	0	224
Dhuna	OBC	31	4	4	0	0	39
Fakir	OBC	1686	285	123	13	3	2110
Gaddi	OBC	49	3	7	1	0	60
Ghosi	OBC	44	6	5	1	0	56
Jhoja	OBC	112	30	3	2	0	147
Kumhar	OBC	14	1	4	0	0	19
Lohar	OBC	901	138	120	14	2	1175

Contd.

		Non-Workers	*Upto 2000*	*2001-5000*	*5001-10000*	*> 10000*	*Total*
Caste	*Categories*	*No.*	*No.*	*No.*	*No.*	*No.*	*No.*
Mahigir	OBC	30	9	1	1	0	41
Manihar	OBC	747	130	82	6	0	965
Mewati	OBC	1549	277	141	15	3	1985
Momin Ansari	OBC	462	117	54	6	2	641
Nai	OBC	69	17	2	0	0	88
Qassab	OBC	787	126	35	11	1	960
Rangrez	OBC	36	3	5	1	0	45
Rayeen	OBC	89	18	8	0	0	115
Sangtarash	OBC	7	2	0	0	0	9
Teli	OBC	617	133	33	8	1	792
Not Specified		108	27	9	2	1	147
	Total	13555	2490	1180	203	53	17481

Income disparity between Muslim General and OBC is evident from the data, presented in the above Table No. 2. Fifty seven per cent workers of General category as against 65 per cent of OBC belong to lowest income group. Although their percentage in the second income group is nearly equal (29.58% General and 30.35% OBCs), disparity of income between them persists in the third income group (8.95% General and 3.63% OBCs) and in the highest income group (3.54% General and 0.44% OBCs). In this way, data of this survey supports findings of PHLC according to which Muslim OBCs are poorer than Muslim General.

Occupations

Occupations are more important than income in a hierarchical society like India. They define social status and affect lifestyle of workers. Manual labour related occupations, no matter whatsoever the income from these occupations is, are considered of low social status. They prevent workers to fully participate in civic life, to pay due attention to the up-bringing of their children and to lead a comfortable life. On the contrary, salaried jobs, trade and commerce and mental labour related occupations are thought to be of higher status and enable workers to avail many opportunities in different spheres of life.

Occupations have long been associated with castes/ *baradaries*. However, no systematic association of caste with occupation is found in contemporary India. Indeed, occupations have largely become caste-free. Nonetheless, occupational pattern of a caste/community is largely determined by the ownership of physical assets like agricultural land and immovable property as well as human assets like education. Being poor, illiterate and powerless community, Muslims are found to be largely concentrated in informal sector as unskilled and skilled workers and under represented in salaried jobs and in mental work related occupations. Many of them are self-employed as vendors, artisans of home based industry, mechanics and so on. In short, Muslims are mostly engaged in occupation of low social status and their economic condition is highly vulnerable (see Chapter-5 of PHLC report, 2006).

Table 3
Occupation-wise Distribution of Workers in Rural and Urban Areas

Occupation	*Rural*	*Rural %*	*Urban*	*Urban %*	*Total*
Administrative/Executive Official	0	0	9	100	9
Agriculture Workers	36	52.17	33	47.83	69
Animal husbandry and related works	16	42.11	22	57.89	38
Bakery	2	25	6	75	8
Bangle/Glass work	86	92.47	7	7.53	93
Barber/Beauty Parlour	5	29.41	12	70.59	17
Beggar	2	66.67	1	33.33	3
Clerical jobs	11	24.44	34	75.56	45
Contractor	1	16.67	5	83.33	6
Cook/Halwai	0	0	10	100	10
Cultivator	147	62.55	88	37.45	235
Customer Care	0	0	1	100	1
Driver/Conductor	57	60	38	40	95
Electrical Fitters/Electrical and Electronic work	3	20	12	80	15
Engineer	0	0	11	100	11
Factory/Industry	10	45.45	12	54.55	22
Gardener	2	28.57	5	71.43	7
Government schemes related workers	0	0	10	100	10
Imam/Hafiz/Moazzin /Moulvi /Theologian	6	66.67	3	33.33	9
Insurance /Investment	0	0	1	100	1
Ironsmith/carpenter/potters	44	45.36	53	54.64	97
Junk dealer	2	14.29	12	85.71	14
Lab Attendant	1	33.33	2	66.67	3

Contd.

Occupation	Rural	Rural %	Urban	Urban %	Total
Lawyer	0	0	2	100	2
Lock work/brass work/metal polish	93	22.96	312	77.04	405
Maid servant	1	33.33	2	66.67	3
Mason and Painter	22	52.38	20	47.62	42
Meat/chicken/fish seller	4	30.77	9	69.23	13
Mechanic	29	29	71	71	100
Merchant/Traders	18	15	102	85	120
Musical band player/singer	0	0	3	100	3
Pensioner	0	0	27	100	27
Plumber	5	31.25	11	68.75	16
Police and armed forces	4	57.14	3	42.86	7
Politician	0	0	1	100	1
Printing	3	50	3	50	6
Qualified Medical Practitioner	4	50	4	50	8
Rag picking	0	0	13	100	13
Rickshaw Puller/Cycle Repairing	43	39.09	67	60.91	110
Salesman	2	10	18	90	20
Shopkeeper	59	29.8	139	70.2	198
Supervisor, Security Guard, Chowkidar	6	10.17	53	89.83	59
Tailoring	62	38.51	99	61.49	161
Tea Stall/Dhaba/Small hotel	6	26.09	17	73.91	23
Tonga/bullock cart	6	75	2	25	8
Transport	3	60	2	40	5
Tutor/teacher	13	26.53	36	73.47	49

Contd.

Occupation	*Rural*	*Rural %*	*Urban*	*Urban %*	*Total*
Unqualified Medical Practitioner	6	37.5	10	62.5	16
Unskilled worker	749	50.17	744	49.83	1493
Vendor	52	32.7	107	67.3	159
Washer man	2	5.88	32	94.12	34
Working in Middle East	0	0	7	100	7
Total	1623	41.34	2303	58.66	3926

Respondents were asked to report the names of occupations in which workers of their households were engaged. Reported occupations are alphabetically arranged in the preceding Table No. 3. However, daily wage earners, (reported as *Mazdoors, Palledars, Beldar, Dehari Mazdoor, Labourwala, Bhatta mazdoor* etc.) other than agricultural workers are enumerated under the category of unskilled workers.

The above Table No. 3 reveals heavy concentration of workers in informal sector of economy. Most of them are either unskilled and skilled workers or are engaged in self employed occupations. Largest number of workers i.e. 1493 (38.03%) are 'Unskilled', followed by 405 (10.32%). lock work/brass work/ metal polish.

Census Classification

Census of India 2001 classify workers into four categories i.e. Cultivators, Agricultural Workers, Household Industry Workers and Other Workers and provides their religion-wise distribution.

Cultivator is defined as a person, who is engaged in cultivation of land owned or held from government or from private person or institutions for payment in money, kind or share while Agricultural Worker is a person, who works on another person's land for wages in money or kind or share. Household Industrial Worker is one who is engaged in production of some artefacts at home. Household industry is not a registered factory. The category of Other Workers (OW) is residual and, therefore, includes all workers other than Cultivators, Agricultural Workers and Household Industry Workers. It includes all government servants, municipal employees, teachers, factory workers, plantation workers, those engaged in trade, commerce, business, transport, banking, mining, construction, political or social work, priests, entertainment artist etc. Hence workers of innumerable kinds having varied socio-economic status in society and life chances in market situations are included in this category.

In order to compare estimate of this survey with the data of Census of India 2001, reported occupations and workers are classified into above mentioned Census categories of workers in the following Table No. 4.

Thus, the data of the survey reveal that highest percentage of workers (79.6%) belong to Census category of Other Workers. Next to them are Household Industrial Workers (12.69%) followed by cultivators (5.99%). Lowest percentage (1.76%) is of Agricultural Workers. Hence survey estimate is at variance with that of Census of India 2001 data according to which 65.37 per cent are Other Workers, 15.56 per cent Household Industrial Workers, 11.13 per cent Cultivators and 7.97 per cent Agricultural Workers among Muslims of district Aligarh. The variation may likely be due to the fact that Census figures are of district whereas survey estimate is of 2500 sample households of *Tehsil Koil*.

Child Labour

Child worker (worker under the age of 14 years) is against the law in India. It is being prohibited by *The Child Labour (Prohibition and Regulation) Act, 1986*. However, child labour is wide spread and found in various sectors of economy such as agriculture, Transport and communication, mining and quarrying, construction, manufacturing, processing, servicing and repairs and so on. Exact data about child labour are not available. Nonetheless, studies and surveys estimate about 80 million child labour in the country. Poverty has been identified as the major cause of child labour. Indeed, a child is an economic asset of a poor household who is to work either as an assistant of his family members or work independently. Hence a child directly and indirectly contributes to the income of household and consequently deprived of childhood and education.

We defined a child worker as a person of 7-14 years age who goes outside the home to work. Those children who assist family members in their work are not defined as child workers. As per this definition 83 (2.11%) child workers in the workforce of 3926 are found. Distribution of child workers across occupations in both rural and urban areas is presented in the Table No. 5.

Table 4
Classification of Reported Workers into Census Categories of Workers

Census Categories	*Occupation*	*Total(Percent)*
Cultivators	Cultivators	235(5.99%)
Agricultural workers	Agriculture Workers	69(1.76%)
Household Industry workers	Lock work/brass work/metal polish	405(10.32%)
	Bangle/Glass work	93(2.37%)
Other Workers	Unskilled worker	1493(38%)
	Shopkeeper	198(5.04%)
	Tailoring	161(4.1%)
	Vendor	159(4.05%)
	Merchant/Traders	120(3.06%)
	Rickshaw Puller/Cycle Repairing	110(2.8%)
	Mechanic	100(2.55%)
	Ironsmith/carpenter/potters	97(2.47%)
	Driver/Conductor	95(2.42%)
	Supervisor, Security Guard,Chowkidar	59(1.5%)
	Tutor/teacher	49(1.25%)
	Clerical jobs	45(1.15%)
	Mason and Painter	42(1.07%)
	Animal husbandry and related works	38(0.97%)
	Washer man	34(0.87%)
	Pensioner	27(0.69%)
	Tea Stall/Dhaba/Small hotel	23(.059%)
	Factory/Industry	22(0.56%)
	Salesman	20(0.51%)

Contd.

Census Categories	*Occupation*	*Total(Percent)*
	Barber/Beauty Parlour	17(0.43%)
	Plumber	16(0.41%)
	Unqualified Medical Practitioner	16(0.41%)
	Electrical Fitters/Electrical and Electronic work	15(0.38%)
	Junk dealer	14(0.36%)
	Meat/chicken/fisher seller	13(0.33%)
	Rag picking	13(0.33%)
	Engineer	11(0.28%)
	Cook/Halwai	10(0.25%)
	Government schemes related workers	10(0.25%)
	Administrative/Executive Official	9(0.23%)
	Imam/Hafiz/Moazzim/Molvi/Theologian	9(0.23%)
	Bakery	8(0.2%)
	Qualified Medical Practitioner	8(0.2%)
	Tonga/bullock cart	8(0.2%)
	Gardener	7(0.18%)
	Police and armed forces	7(0.18%)
	Working in Middle East	7(0.18%)
	Contractor	6(0.15%)
	Printing	6(0.15%)
	Transport	5(0.13%)
	Beggar	3(0.08%)
	Lab Attendant	3(0.08%)
	Maid servant	3(0.08%)
	Musical band player/singer	3(0.08%)

Contd.

Census Categories	*Occupation*	*Total(Percent)*
	Lawyer	2(0.05%)
	Customer Care	1(0.03%)
	Insurance/Investment	1(0.03%)
	Politician	1(0.03%)
	Total	3926(100%)

Table 5
Occupation-wise Distribution of Child Workers in Rural and Urban Areas

Occupation	*Rural*	*Urban*	*Total*
Bangle/Glass work	2	0	2
Driver/Conductor	0	1	1
Agricultural Labourer	1	0	1
Ironsmith/carpenter/potters	1	1	2
Junk dealer	0	3	3
Lock work/brass work/metal polish	1	14	15
Mason and Painter	1	0	1
Mechanic	0	1	1
Rag picking	0	7	7
Shopkeeper	0	1	1
Tailoring	2	5	7
Unskilled worker	19	21	40
Washer man	0	2	2
Total	27	56	83

It is revealed by the above Table No. 5 that child workers are more in urban areas i.e. 56 (67.47%) than in villages 27 (32.53%). Highest percentage (48.19%) is of unskilled workers, followed by lock work/brass work/metal polish (18.07%).

As the estimate of the survey reveals 3926 workers in a population of 17481, WPR is 22 per cent, 8 percentage point below to the district average. Most of the workers belong to lowest income group and economically vulnerable occupations.

Village workers are found to be poorer than urban workers as 73 per cent of former and 58 per cent of latter belong to lowest income group. Income disparity between Muslim General and OBCs is conspicuous. For 57 per cent workers of General category and 65 per cent of OBC belong to lowest income group. More than 2 per cent of total workers are children under the age of 14 years who are found both in rural and in urban areas.

5

Literacy and Education

Education is the most critical indicator of human development and a pre-requisite of socio-economic progress. "Improvements in the functional and analytical ability of children and youth through education open up opportunities leading to both individual and group entitlements. Improvements in education are not only expected to enhance efficiency (and therefore earnings) but also augment democratic participation, upgrade health and quality of life." (GoI 2006: 49). However, millions of children and youth are deprived of education in India despite Constitutional commitment and legal enactment to provide free and compulsory education to all children up to the age of 14 years. Among all socio-religious communities Muslims are most educationally deprived community of the country. This chapter presents data related with literacy rate, level of traditional and modern education, gender education, dropouts etc. It also looks into educational status across *Baradaries*.

Literacy

Literacy remains most commonly understood primary indicator of educational status despite its many inadequacies. It is defined in Census operations as the ability of a person to read and write with understanding in any language. A person who can merely read but cannot write is not classified as literate. Any formal education or minimum educational standard is not necessary to be considered literate. Census excludes population of 0-6 years age from the calculation of literacy rate. It is appropriate here to underline the fact that, "many so-called literates did not have the ability to apply their reading and writing skills to real life situations, and often a substantial proportion reverted to illiteracy within 4-5 years after leaving school. This aspect is not taken into account by the Census definition." (GoI 2006:50-51).

While using the Census definition of literacy, population (excluding 0-6 years) of surveyed households i.e. 14,166 is classified into illiterates and literates and presented in the Table No. 1 given below.

Table 1
Literacy in Rural and Urban Areas

	Illiterate			*Literate*			
Categories	*Male*	*Female*	*Total*	*Male*	*Female*	*Total*	*Total*
Rural	1407	1839	3246	1673	984	2657	5903
Urban	1752	2236	3988	2567	1708	4275	8263
Total	3159	4075	7234	4240	2692	6932	14166

It is evident from the above Table No. 1 that there are 7234 illiterates and 6932 literates. Hence literacy rate is 49 per cent, 9 percentage points below to average literacy rate of district Aligarh in 2001. A gap of 6.7 percentage points exists between rural and urban areas as 45 per cent people of rural households as against 51.17 per cent of urban households are found literate. Similar gap exists between females and males. Females are 17.52 percentage points behind males in literacy. Their literacy rate is 39.78 per cent as against 57.30 per cent of males. Although 17.52 per cent gender gap in literacy is quite wide, it is less than district average which is 28.68 per cent.

Never Attended School/Madrasa Literates

It is mentioned above that formal education of a person is not a condition for defining him/her a literate person. A person can acquire knowledge of reading and writing in any language without going to school. Generally such knowledge is acquired in the family or at work place. Number of never attended school/Madrasa literates are shown in the following Table 2.

Table 2
Never Attended School/Madrasa Literates

Categories	*Male*	*Male %*	*Female*	*Female %*	*Total*
Rural	20	37.74	33	62.26	53
Urban	37	31.9	79	68.1	116
Total	57	33.73	112	66.27	169

It is evident from the above Table No. 2 that 169 (2.43%) of the total literate persons have never attended educational institutions. Number of such literates are more in urban areas (116) than villages (53). It is important to note that number of female literates without school or Madrasa education are two times more (112) than males (57). It indicates that Muslim families impart basic education to their females more than that of males at home.

Education

Type of Education

Education is classified into three categories i.e. Madrasa, Modern and both Madrasa and Modern education for the purpose of this survey. Madrasa (Pl-Madaris) is a faith based educational institution, imparting both religious education and elementary knowledge of secular education. Modern education is imparted by schools and colleges which mainly focus on structured non-religious education. These types of education among literates excluding never attended school/Madrasa literates, numbering 6763 are presented in the following Table No. 3.

It is evident from the Table No. 3 that 85.27 per cent (6763) have Only modern education whereas 3.36 per cent (227) are found having Only Madrasa education. Remaining 11.37 per cent (769) literates have both modern and Madrasa education. Indeed, many Muslims initiate their education from Madrasa and later on shift to modern education. Thus, they have both Madrasa and modern education.

Table 3
Type of Education

	Rural					*Urban*						
Literacy Status	*Male*	*Male %*	*Female*	*Female %*	*Total*	*Male*	*Male %*	*Female*	*Female %*	*Total*	*Total*	*%*
Modern Education	1443	68.49	664	31.51	2107	2273	62.1	1387	37.9	3660	5767	85.27
Madrasa Education	24	22.02	85	77.98	109	56	47.46	62	52.54	118	227	3.36
Both Modern & Madrasa	186	47.94	202	52.06	388	201	52.76	180	47.24	381	769	11.37
Total	1653	63.48	951	36.52	2604	2530	60.83	1629	39.17	4159	6763	100

Rural-urban and gender gap is visible in both modern and Madrasa education. Eighty per cent villagers as against 88 per cent urban dwellers have only modern education. Percentage of Only Madrasa educated is more among villagers (4.19%) than people of urban areas (2.84%). Females are found behind males in modern education as 79.5 per cent of them as against 88.84 per cent males have only modern education. Percentage of females having only Madrasa education is three times more than that of males (Male- 1.91% and Female- 5.7%).

Madrasa Education

Madaris are of various kinds and, therefore, impart different level of education. Respondents are asked to report highest level of Madrasa education of 996 persons, (227 only Madrasa educated and 769 of both modern and Madrasa educated). Their responses are shown in the following Table No. 4.

Highest percentage (87.15%) is of those who have *Nazra* level Madrasa education. *Nazra* is a course of Quran reading in Arabic without any understanding of Arabic language. This is followed by *Maktab* level education (6.63%). *Maktab* is a primary Madrasa which imparts religious and secular elementary education. *Hafiz* (A person who is taught to memorize the Quran) are 36 (3.61%) whereas very few persons are found to be *Aalim* (10), *Munshi* (2), *Fazil*(2), *Muallim*(2).

Madrasa boards of various state recognize degree of *Munshi*, *Alim* and *Fazil* equivalent to High School, Intermediate and graduation level of Modern education respectively. Certificate of *Adeeb* (equivalent to High School) is not awarded by Madrasa but by Jamia Urdu Aligarh, an institution established to promote modern education in Urdu medium.

Baradaries and Madrasa Education

Madrasa educated persons (numbering 996) across their *Baradaries* are shown in following Table No. 5.

Of the total Madrasa educated persons among Muslim General, as shown in the Table No. 6, Eighty-five per cent have *Nazra* level education, followed by *Maktab* (6.76%), *Hafiz* (4.59%), *Aalim* (1.89%), *Adeeb* (1.35%) and *Muallim* (0.54%).

Table 4
Level of Madrasa Education

Categories	*Nazra*		*Maktab*		*Hafiz*		*Munshi*		*Alim*		*Fazil*		*Adeeb*		*Muallim*	
	Male	*Female*	*Male*	*Female*	*Male*	*Female*	*Male*	*Female*	*Male*	*Female*	*Male*	*Female*	*Male*	*Female*	*Male*	*Female*
Rural	189	265	13	19	6	1	0	0	0	0	1	0	0	2	1	0
Urban	190	224	23	11	28	1	2	0	8	2	1	0	5	3	0	1
Total	379	489	36	30	34	2	2	0	8	2	2	0	5	5	1	1

Table 5

***Baradari*-wise Madrasa Education**

Baradaries	Category	*Nazra*		*Maktab*		*Hafiz*		*Munsi*		*Alim*		*Fazil*		*Adeeb*		*Muallim*	
		Male	*Female*	*Male*	*Female*	*Male*	*Female*	*Male*	*Female*	*Male*	*Female*	*Male*	*Female*	*Male*	*Female*	*Male*	*Female*
Farooqui	General	0	0	0	0	0	0	0	0	0	0	0	0	0	0	0	0
Mughal	General	5	8	4	2	0	0	0	0	0	0	0	0	0	0	0	0
Pathan	General	28	42	3	4	3	0	0	0	0	0	0	0	1	0	0	1
Rajput	General	95	102	5	4	2	1	0	0	4	0	0	0	0	2	1	0
Shamshi	General	1	3	0	0	0	0	0	0	0	0	0	0	0	0	0	0
Sheikh	General	7	14	0	0	8	1	0	0	2	1	0	0	1	1	0	0
Syed	General	4	5	2	1	2	0	0	0	0	0	0	0	0	0	0	0
Warsi	General	0	0	0	0	0	0	0	0	0	0	0	0	0	0	0	0
Total (General)		140	174	14	11	15	2	0	0	6	1	0	0	2	3	1	1
Banjara	OBC	0	0	0	0	0	0	0	0	0	0	0	0	0	0	0	0
Bawarchi	OBC	0	0	0	0	0	0	0	0	0	0	0	0	0	0	0	0
Bhisti	OBC	45	43	5	7	5	0	0	0	1	0	1	0	1	0	0	0
Bhurji	OBC	1	1	0	0	0	0	0	0	0	0	0	0	0	0	0	0
Chunpat	OBC	0	0	0	0	0	0	0	0	0	0	0	0	0	0	0	0
Darzi	OBC	2	0	0	0	1	0	0	0	0	0	0	0	0	0	0	0
Dhobi	OBC	0	2	0	0	0	0	0	0	0	0	0	0	0	0	0	0
Dhuna	OBC	1	0	0	0	0	0	0	0	0	0	0	0	0	0	0	0
Fakir	OBC	25	42	0	2	4	0	0	0	0	0	1	0	0	0	0	0
Gaddi	OBC	1	3	0	0	0	0	0	0	0	0	0	0	0	0	0	0
Ghosi	OBC	1	1	0	0	0	0	0	0	0	0	0	0	0	0	0	0
Jhoja	OBC	1	0	0	0	0	0	0	0	0	0	0	0	0	0	0	0
Kumhar	OBC	0	0	0	0	0	0	0	0	0	0	0	0	0	0	0	0
Lohar	OBC	46	38	6	2	1	0	0	0	0	0	0	0	1	1	0	0
Mahigir	OBC	0	0	0	0	0	0	0	0	0	0	0	0	0	0	0	0
Manihar	OBC	28	66	0	3	1	0	0	0	0	0	0	0	0	0	0	0
Mewati	OBC	41	46	5	4	2	0	2	0	0	0	0	0	1	1	0	0

Contd.

Baradaries	*Category*	*Nazra*		*Maktab*		*Hafiz*		*Munsi*		*Alim*		*Fazil*		*Adeeb*		*Muallim*	
		Male	*Female*	*Male*	*Female*	*Male*	*Female*	*Male*	*Female*	*Male*	*Female*	*Male*	*Female*	*Male*	*Female*	*Male*	*Female*
Momin Ansari	OBC	9	11	1	0	2	0	0	0	1	0	0	0	0	0	0	0
Nai	OBC	0	5	0	0	1	0	0	0	0	0	0	0	0	0	0	0
Qassab	OBC	17	33	2	1	0	0	0	0	0	1	0	0	0	0	0	0
Rangrez	OBC	0	0	0	0	0	0	0	0	0	0	0	0	0	0	0	0
Rayeen	OBC	3	4	0	0	0	0	0	0	0	0	0	0	0	0	0	0
Sangtarash	OBC	0	0	0	0	0	0	0	0	0	0	0	0	0	0	0	0
Teli	OBC	17	18	3	0	2	0	0	0	0	0	0	0	0	0	0	0
Total (OBC)		238	313	22	19	19	0	2	0	2	1	2	0	3	2	0	0
Not Specified		1	2	0	0	0	0	0	0	0	0	0	0	0	0	0	0
G. Total		379	489	36	30	34	2	2	0	8	2	2	0	5	5	1	1

Muslim OBCs are ahead to Muslim General by 4 percentage points at *Nazra* level education whereas their percentage at *Maktab* level education (6.58%) is almost equal to Muslim General. However, Muslim OBCs are behind to Muslim General at higher level of Madrasa education. For instance they are behind by 1.5 percentage points in both the categories of *Hafiz* and *Alim*.

Modern Education

Highest level of modern education among those, having only modern education (5767) and both Madrasa and Modern education (769) is presented in the following Table No. 6. Persons having technical/professional education are also counted in school graduate, and postgraduate level education.

Primary education emerges from the above Table No. 6 as the highest level of education among 45.88 per cent people which is followed by Junior level education (24.86%). Percentage of people consistently declines with the increase in the level of education. Therefore, 17.43%, 7.47%, 3.03% and 1.33% persons are found having High School, Intermediate, Graduate, and Post-graduate level education respectively. Such an educational trend, though worrisome, is not surprising. It is an all India phenomenon among Muslims. PHLC 2006, reports that, "Muslims are at a double disadvantage with low levels of education combined with low quality education; their deprivation increases manifold as the level of education rises" (GoI 2006: 50).

Technical/Professional Education

Condition of technical/professional education, vital for employment, is worst among Muslims. Only 135 persons, as shown in the above Table No. 6, are found to have various kinds of technical/professional education. Their highest level of education is presented in the Table No. 7.

One hundred thirty five persons, as shown in Table No. 7, have 39 types of technical/professional education. Their largest numbers appear to have Certificate/Diploma level education. Only 26 females and 21 persons of rural households are found

Table 6
Level of Modern Education

Categories	Primary (Upto V)		Junior (VI-VIII)		High School (IX-X)		Intermediate (XI-XII)		Graduation		Post Graduation		Professional/ Technical Education	
	Male	Female	Male	Female	Male	Female	Male	Female	Male	Female	Male	Female	Male	Female
Rural	769	533	431	231	299	58	100	35	20	7	10	2	18	3
Urban	1017	680	588	375	498	284	225	128	101	70	45	30	91	23
Total	1786	1213	1019	606	797	342	325	163	121	77	55	32	109	26

Table 7
Technical/Professional Education

Professional/Technical Education	*Rural*			*Urban*			*Grand Total*
	Male	*Female*	*Total*	*Male*	*Female*	*Total*	
B.A.LLB	0	0	0	1	0	1	1
B.E	1	0	1	0	0	0	1
B.Ed.	1	0	1	3	3	6	7
B.Lib.	1	0	1	1	2	3	4
B.P.T	1	0	1	0	0	0	1
B.Tech.	2	1	3	12	0	12	15
B.U.M.S.	3	0	3	3	7	10	13
BAMS	0	0	0	1	0	1	1
BBA	0	0	0	0	2	2	2
BCA	0	0	0	2	0	2	2
BDS	0	0	0	1	0	1	1
BE	0	0	0	2	1	3	3
BEMS	1	0	1	0	0	0	1
BTC	1	0	1	1	0	1	2
Certificate in Food Craft	1	0	1	0	0	0	1
CFA	0	0	0	2	0	2	2
Computer Course	0	0	0	3	0	3	3
D.C.A.	0	0	0	2	0	2	2
D.M.L.T	1	0	1	0	0	0	1
DBA	0	0	0	1	0	1	1
Dip. in Food Production	0	0	0	1	0	1	1
Dip. Costume Designing	0	0	0	0	1	1	1

Contd.

Professional/Technical Education	*Rural*			*Urban*			*Grand Total*
	Male	*Female*	*Total*	*Male*	*Female*	*Total*	
Dip. Engg.	1	0	1	20	2	22	23
DMLT	1	0	1	1	0	1	2
Dye Cutting	0	0	0	1	0	1	2
Hotel Management	0	0	0	2	0	2	2
ITI	2	0	2	10	0	10	12
L.L.B.	0	0	0	6	0	6	6
M.Lib.	0	1	1	0	1	1	2
M.Sc. Ag	1	0	1	0	0	0	1
M.Tech.	0	0	0	3	0	3	3
MBA	0	0	0	5	0	5	5
MBBS	0	0	0	3	0	3	3
MCA	0	0	0	1	1	2	2
MTA	0	0	0	1	0	1	1
OASP	0	0	0	0	1	1	1
Office Management	0	0	0	0	1	1	1
P.G.D.C.A.	0	1	1	1	1	2	3
PGIR&PM	0	0	0	1	0	1	1
Total	18	3	21	91	23	114	135
M.Sc. Ag	1	0	1	0	0	0	1
M.Tech.	0	0	0	3	0	3	3
MBA	0	0	0	5	0	5	5
MBBS	0	0	0	3	0	3	3
MCA	0	0	0	1	1	2	2

Contd.

Professional/Technical Education	Rural			Urban			Grand Total
	Male	Female	Total	Male	Female	Total	
MTA	0	0	0	1	0	1	1
OASP	0	0	0	0	1	1	1
Office Management	0	0	0	0	1	1	1
P.G.D.C.A.	0	1	1	1	1	2	3
PGIR&PM	0	0	0	1	0	1	1
Total	18	3	21	91	23	114	135

having technical/professional education. Therefore, rural-urban and gender gap is very wide in this type of education.

Baradaries and Modern Education

Baradari-wise distribution of 6536 persons, having acquired different level of modern education, is shown in the following Table No. 8.

Table No. 8 reveals that 2219 Muslim General and 4288 Muslim OBCs have different level of modern education. Thirty-five per cent Muslim General and 51 per cent OBCs have Primary level education. Hence former are behind the latter by 15 percentage points at Primary level education. The gap has become almost equal at Junior level of education (Muslim General- 23.97% and OBCs- 25.33%). Nonetheless, Muslim OBCs remain consistently behind Muslim General at all remaining level of education. The gap between them is of 5 percentage points at the level of High School which goes up to 6 percentage points at Intermediate level. It declines to 4 percentage points at Graduate level and 2 percentage points at the post-graduate level of education. Thus the data explicitly show that retention rate of Muslim OBCs in High School onwards level education is below to that of Muslim General.

The gap between Muslim General and OBCs widens in technical/professional education. Out of 135 persons, having acquired technical/professional education, only 37 are Muslim OBCs.

Attitudes to and Expectations from Modern Education

Educational backwardness of Muslims is, indeed, a complex phenomenon persisting due to external and internal factors. Lack of schools, absence of schools of quality education and indifferent attitudes of Government agencies in the implementation of educational and welfare schemes in Muslim concentration localities as well as deprivation from policies of affirmative action are some of the major external factors. Embedded poverty, negligible professional middle class and feeling of hopelessness or discrimination are few examples of internal factors. These and other factors are generally ignored

Table 8
***Baradari*-wise Level of Modern Education**

Baradaries	Category	Primary (Upto V)		Junior (VI-VIII)		High School (IX-X)		Intermediate (XI-XII)		Graduation		Post Graduation		Professional/ Technical Education	
		Male	*Female*	*Male*	*Female*	*Male*	*Female*	*Male*	*Female*	*Male*	*Female*	*Male*	*Female*	*Male*	*Female*
Farooqui	General	0	0	0	1	1	0	0	0	0	0	0	0	0	0
Mughal	General	27	15	8	8	8	3	2	1	0	1	1	1	1	1
Pathan	General	159	132	113	80	80	74	48	32	16	13	10	10	21	3
Rajput	General	207	173	142	104	116	31	58	22	18	8	5	1	14	1
Shamshi	General	2	1	0	1	4	1	0	3	0	2	0	0	0	1
Sheikh	General	38	23	30	23	44	32	21	15	17	16	12	9	14	13
Syed	General	18	6	15	7	30	27	30	19	16	17	3	3	22	6
Warsi	General	0	0	0	0	0	2	1	1	1	0	0	0	0	0
Total (General)		451	350	308	224	283	170	160	93	68	57	31	24	72	25
Banjara	OBC	1	0	0	0	0	0	0	0	0	0	0	0	0	0
Bawarchi	OBC	1	0	0	0	0	0	0	0	0	0	0	0	0	0
Bhisti	OBC	301	175	162	80	120	32	34	10	5	3	3	0	5	0
Bhurji	OBC	26	10	14	3	4	0	1	0	0	1	0	0	0	0
Chunpat	OBC	3	0	2	0	0	1	0	1	0	1	0	0	0	0
Darzi	OBC	13	8	6	2	4	1	0	1	0	0	0	0	0	0
Dhobi	OBC	13	7	11	11	7	0	0	1	0	0	0	0	0	0
Dhuna	OBC	3	3	1	6	3	2	0	1	0	0	0	0	0	0
Fakir	OBC	214	122	82	39	60	16	16	4	5	2	0	0	5	0
Gaddi	OBC	3	1	8	0	1	2	1	0	0	2	0	0	0	0
Ghosi	OBC	1	3	2	0	1	0	0	0	0	0	0	0	0	0
Jhoja	OBC	14	5	10	3	6	1	5	2	2	0	1	1	0	0
Kumhar	OBC	0	0	0	0	0	0	0	0	0	0	0	0	0	0

Contd.

Baradaries	*Category*	*Primary (Upto V)*		*Junior (VI-VIII)*		*High School (IX-X)*		*Intermediate (XI-XII)*		*Graduation*		*Post Graduation*		*Professional/ Technical Education*	
		Male	*Female*	*Male*	*Female*	*Male*	*Female*	*Male*	*Female*	*Male*	*Female*	*Male*	*Female*	*Male*	*Female*
Lohar	OBC	129	115	77	49	73	38	28	13	13	4	8	2	11	1
Mahigir	OBC	6	3	1	0	1	0	0	1	0	0	0	0	0	0
Manihar	OBC	127	81	64	36	46	6	16	10	3	0	0	0	1	0
Mewati	OBC	196	120	103	41	57	20	22	9	5	0	2	0	2	0
Momin Ansari	OBC	69	49	31	32	28	20	9	7	7	3	5	3	5	0
Nai	OBC	9	8	4	5	5	1	2	0	1	1	0	0	0	0
Qassab	OBC	91	67	59	26	32	20	9	2	6	1	1	1	2	0
Rangrez	OBC	11	4	4	5	3	1	1	1	1	0	0	0	0	0
Rayeen	OBC	13	4	1	1	0	2	0	0	0	0	0	0	0	0
Sangtarash	OBC	1	0	0	0	1	0	0	0	0	0	0	0	0	0
Teli	OBC	88	75	63	42	59	6	17	5	2	2	3	0	5	0
Total (OBC)		1333	860	705	381	511	169	161	68	50	20	23	7	36	1
Not Specified		2	3	6	1	3	3	4	2	3	0	1	1	1	0
G. Total		1786	1213	1019	606	797	342	325	163	121	77	55	32	109	26

in the analysis of Muslim's educational backwardness and they are simply being pictured as a conservative community which likes to remain illiterate. On the contrary, Muslims long for acquiring education as per the data of this survey. Respondents were asked about their attitudes towards modern education and the expectation from it. These questions and their answers are presented in the Table No. 9.

Table 9
Attitudes Towards Modern Education

	No. of Households	
Attitude and Response on Education	*Yes*	*No*
Education is necessary for Muslim uplift	2452	48
Education as good investment	2462	38
Prospects of employment after good school education	2372	128
Education greater than high school is only for job	2107	393
Total	9393	607

All Respondent except 48 (1.92%) considers education as a key for Muslim uplift. All of them excluding 38 (1.52%) consider education as a good investment. Education greater than High School is linked with employment by 2107 (84.28%) Respondents while 2372 (94.88%) Respondents think that prospects of employment increases if a person has good school education. Thus it is evident that factors of Muslim educational backwardness are other than their attitudes towards education. They are not hopeless with education. Their educational status may considerably be improved in near future if they are provided with good opportunities which are, indeed, not available to many of them.

In a nutshell, estimates of this survey exhibit 49 per cent literacy rate among people of surveyed households which is 9 percentage points below to district average. Villagers, having 45 per cent literacy rate, are 6 percentage points behind to urban dwellers. A gap of 17.52 percentage points exists between males (57.28%) and females (39.78%) in literacy rate which is 11 percentage points below to district average.

Of the total literate population (excluding never attended school/Madrasa literates) 85 per cent have 'Only Modern' education of different levels whereas 11.37 per cent have both 'Madrasa and Modern' education. Merely 3.36 per cent literates are found having 'Only Madrasa' education.

The phenomenon of decreasing numbers with increasing level of education is conspicuous in both Madrasa and Modern education. Thus 45 per cent of those who acquired Only Modern education and both Modern and Madrasa education have Primary level education. The percentage sharply comes down to 17.4 per cent at Junior level education and remains consistently declining at all level of education. It is merely 1.33 per cent at Post-graduate level. The condition of technical/ professional education is worst as only 135 persons are reported to have this kind of education.

Gender and rural-urban gap in all type of education is visible in the data. Gap also exists between Muslim General and OBCs. Former lag behind the later at lowest level of both Madrasa and Modern education. However, they are ahead to the later at higher level of Madrasa and Modern education as well as technical/professional education.

6

Schools and Madaris

A survey of 89 schools and 34 Madaris is conducted along with household survey to explore the kind of education available to Muslims in their neighbourhood. The survey covers all schools/Madaris of sampled villages. Whereas, selected schools/Madaris of urban areas, located in sampled localities and in their Muslim concentrated neighbourhood, are surveyed (List of Schools-Annexure:III and List of Madaris-Annexure: IV). Information are reported by Principal of a school or *Mohtamim* of a Madrasa.

Type of Schools

Surveyed schools are of following categories

Primary only (From Class-I to Class-V)	60
Upper Primary only (From Class-VI to Class VIII)	6
Primary with Upper Primary (From Class-I to Class-VIII)	21
Primary with Upper Primary and Secondary/Higher Secondary (From class I to Class- XII)	2
Total	89

Thus, it is explicit that number of schools decline as the level of education goes up. There are only two schools, providing Secondary and Senior Secondary level education.

All schools are private except 13 only Primary and 5 only Upper Primary Government schools. Hence Government contribution in promoting school education in Muslim concentration areas is only of symbolic importance. Out of 13 only Primary Government schools, 8 are located in villages while remaining are in urban areas. No only Primary government school exists in villages. Thus, Muslim villagers do not have access to school education higher than Primary level which is even not available to one of the surveyed villages.

Out of 71 privately managed schools, 65(Primary only-42, Only Upper Primary-1, Primary with Upper Primary - 21, and Upper Primary with Secondary and Senior Secondary-1) are Muslim managed while remaining are managed by non-Muslims.

Gender and Medium of Instruction

Schools are further classified on the basis of gender i.e. Only boys, Only girls and co-educational and also on the basis of medium of instruction. i.e. Hindi. English and Urdu. Government, Muslims and Non-Muslim Managed schools are separately shown in the following Tables Nos. 1, 2 and 3 across above mentioned indicators.

Out of 89 schools, as shown in Tables Nos. 1, 2 and 3, eighty-three are co-educational while 5 are only for girls, merely one school is only for boys. In this way, number of schools available for girls are more than those available for boys. It is commonly believed that Muslims do not like co-education. This perception is contrary to the data of the survey which unambiguously show that Muslims do not discriminate between boys and girls in school education. Out of 65 Muslim managed schools 63 are co-educational and two are only for girls. Thus Muslim girls have slightly greater access to school education than boys.

Constitution of India enjoins the State to provide elementary education in mother tongue. Both Central and State governments, in pursuance of this Constitutional injunction, formulated policies in this regard which, however, are not followed in practice mainly in the case of Urdu language. An Urdu teacher, as per government policy, is to be provided to every school in which 25 per cent or more students are Muslims. Such a policy is not translated into reality as none of the government school is found to be Urdu medium. Even

Table 1
Government Schools: Nature, Medium of Instruction and Residential Character

Type of School	*Nature of School*			*Medium*			*Residential*
	Boys	*Girls*	*Co-education*	*English*	*Hindi*	*Urdu*	
Primary Only	1	2	10	0	13	0	0
Primary with Upper Primary	0	0	0	0	0	0	0
Primary with Upper Pri. and Sec./Hr. Sec.	0	0	0	0	0	0	0
Upper Primary Only	0	1	4	0	5	0	0
Upper Primary with Sec./Hr. Sec	0	0	0	0	0	0	0
Total	1	3	14	0	18	0	0

Table 2
Private Muslim Managed Schools: Nature, Medium of Instruction and Residential Character

Type of School	*Nature of School*			*Medium*			*Residential*
	Boys	*Girls*	*Co-education*	*English*	*Hindi*	*Urdu*	
Primary Only	0	1	41	21	17	4	0
Primary with Upper Primary	0	1	20	16	4	1	0
Primary with Upper Pri. and Sec./Hr. Sec.	0	0	1	0	1	0	0
Upper Primary Only	0	0	1	1	0	0	0
Upper Primary with Sec./Hr. Sec	0	0	0	0	0	0	0
Total	0	2	63	38	22	5	0

Table 3
Private Non-Muslim Managed: Nature, Medium of Instruction and Residential Character

	Nature of School			*Medium*			
Type of School	*Boys*	*Girls*	*Co-education*	*English*	*Hindi*	*Urdu*	*Residential*
Primary Only	0	0	5	0	5	0	0
Primary with Upper Primary	0	0	0	0	0	0	0
Primary with Upper Pri. And Sec./Hr. Sec.	0	0	1	0	1	0	0
Upper Primary Only	0	0	0	0	0	0	0
Upper Primary with Sec./Hr. Sec	0	0	0	0	0	0	0
Total	0	0	6	0	6	0	0

Urdu is not taught as a subject in these schools despite majority of students have Urdu as their mother tongue.

Status of Urdu is also not good in Muslim managed schools. Out of 65 Muslim managed only 5 are Urdu medium. In remaining schools due attention is not paid to the learning of Urdu language.

School Condition

Condition of Government, Muslim and non-Muslim managed schools is separately shown in the following Tables Nos. 4, 5 and 6.

Table 4
Facilities in Government Schools

Facilities	*Primary Only*	*Primary with Upper Primary*	*Primary with Upper Pri. and Sec./Hr. Sec.*	*Upper Primary Only*	*Upper Primary with Sec./Hr. Sec*
School Building (Owned)	11	0	0	4	0
School Building (Rented)	2	0	0	1	0
Drinking water within school	10	0	0	4	0
Electricity	0	0	0	0	0
Playground	8	0	0	4	0
Boundary wall	7	0	0	2	0
Toilet	12	0	0	5	0
Computers	0	0	0	2	0

One of the aims of Sarva Shiksha Abhiyan (SSA), a mega scheme of Central Government launched in 2001, is to provide useful, relevant and quality elementary education to all children in the age group 7-14 years by 2010. However, many children still do not have access to elementary education. Moreover, useful and quality education remains a distant dream for children who are fortunate enough to enrol themselves in Government managed schools.

Quality of education in Government schools can easily be imagined from the infrastructural facilities available to them, presented in the above Table No. 4. It is evident that three

Table 5
Facilities in Muslim Managed Schools

Facilities	*Primary Only*	*Primary with Upper Primary*	*Primary with Upper Pri. and Sec./Hr. Sec.*	*Upper Primary Only*	*Upper Primary with Sec./Hr. Sec*
School Building (Owned)	3	0	0	0	0
School Building (Rented	2	1	0	0	0
Drinking water within school	4	1	0	0	0
Electricity	4	1	0	0	0
Playground	3	1	0	0	0
Boundary wall	4	1	0	0	0
Toilet	4	1	0	0	0
Computers	1	0	0	0	0

Table 6
Facilities in Non-Muslim Managed Schools

Facilities	*Primary Only*	*Primary with Upper Primary*	*Primary with Upper Pri. and Sec./Hr. Sec.*	*Upper Primary Only*	*Upper Primary with Sec./Hr. Sec*
School Building (Owned)	3	0	0	0	0
School Building (Rented	2	1	0	0	0
Drinking water within school	4	1	0	0	0
Electricity	4	1	0	0	0
Playground	3	1	0	0	0
Boundary wall	4	1	0	0	0
Toilet	4	1	0	0	0
Computer Lab	1	0	0	0	0

schools of Government out of 18 do not have their own building. Basic facilities such as drinking water, toilet, electricity etc., are pre-requisite for opening Government schools under SSA which are not available to all schools. Half of the schools do not have boundary walls. Playground exists in 12 schools but are not properly managed. All schools have separate toilets for boys and girls but are not allowed to be used by students. Facility of drinking water is available in 14 schools and none of the school is found to have the supply of electricity. Computers are reported merely in two schools which are found to be non-functional due to a) non-supply of electricity and b) no computer trained teacher.

Condition of private schools, though better than Government schools, is also worst as it can be seen in the above Table No. 5. Out of 65 Muslim managed schools 17 schools are located in rented building. Ten schools are without boundary walls and half of the schools do not have playground. Facility of drinking water is available in all schools except one and five schools do not have electricity. Separate toilet for boys and girls exists in all school except 5 and are found functional for students. Computers are reported in 16 schools.

Quality of education in these schools cannot be described satisfactory or good. Class room of these schools are over-crowded; teachers are generally under paid and many of them are unqualified. In short, a vast majority of Muslim students do not have access to quality education.

Students' Performance

Performance of students in terminal class examination of Primary (Class-V), and Upper Primary (Class-VIII), level education are shown in the following Table Nos. 7, 8.

It is shown in Table No. 7 that 968 students appeared in class-V examination. Eighty-nine per cent of them passed the examination. Sixty per cent and above marks were secured by 39 per cent students. Comparison of Muslim with non-Muslim students shows that 88 per cent former as against 93 per cent latter passed the examination. However, percentage of students securing 60 and above per cent marks is more among Muslims (41%) than non-Muslims (26%)

Number of students appeared in class eight examination decline to 860. Eighty-three per cent of them passed the examination whereas 60 per cent and above marks were secured by 49 per cent students. Eighty-four per cent of Muslim students and 82 per cent of non-Muslim students passed the examination. In this way, performance of Muslim and non-Muslim students in class-V and VIII examination is nearly equal.

Table 7
Performance of Students in Class V Examination in Only Primary Level School

Examination Report of Last Academic Session											
No. of Students Appearing				*No. of Students Passed*				*No. of Students Getting 60% or Above*			
Muslim		*Non-Muslim*		*Muslim*		*Non- Muslim*		*Muslim*		*Non-Muslim*	
Male	*Female*	*Male*	*Female*	*Male*	*Female*	*Male*	*Female*	*Male*	*Female*	*Male*	*Female*
446	384	77	61	398	335	72	56	158	141	18	15

Table 8
Performance of Students in Class VIII Examination in Primary with Upper Primary Level Schools

Examination Report of Last Academic Session											
No. of Students Appearing				*No. of Students Passed*				*No. of Students Getting 60% or Above*			
Muslim		*Non-Muslim*		*Muslim*		*Non- Muslim*		*Muslim*		*Non-Muslim*	
Male	*Female*	*Male*	*Female*	*Male*	*Female*	*Male*	*Female*	*Male*	*Female*	*Male*	*Female*
321	369	89	81	262	316	74	66	129	157	36	29

Type of Madaris

Madrasa (Pl: Madaris) is an Arabic word, meaning an institution of imparting/acquiring knowledge and skill. It is like a 'school attached to church', provides both religious and secular education. Madrasa came into existence with the establishment of Muslim rule in India. Before colonial period hundreds of Madaris were established with the support of the state and community in different parts of the country. They provided both religious and secular education and contributed immensely in the development of arts, culture, science and other fields of knowledge. Some of the known historical figures like Sher Shah Suri, Abul Fazl Faizi, Todar Mal and Raja Ram Mohan Roy were the product of Madrasa education system.

Madrasa underwent transformation from an institution of religious and secular education to minority institution of religious education. Indeed, Madrasa movement was launched during colonial regime for protecting Muslim identity and promoting religious education. As a result, thousands of Madaris of various kinds were established by Muslims in the country. Their primary aim is to provide religious education. However, many Madaris include secular subjects like Science and Mathematics in their curriculum.

Madaris can be classified into three broad categories i.e. Maktab, Madrasa and Jamia. Maktab is a primary level institution, provides elementary education of both religious and secular subjects whereas Madrasa may be described an institution of secondary level institution. Jamia is an institution of higher learning.

Four kinds of subjects are generally taught in Madaris. These are as follows: a). Language/Literature, b). Contemporary learning, c). Commentary and discourse and d). Law and Jurisprudence. In the language section, Urdu, Persian, Arabic languages and literatures and at places Hindi and English are taught in various Madrasa. In contemporary learning, Mathematics, General Sciences, Hygiene, Geography, History, Economics, Political Science and Philosophy are taught. In the third category, *Sarf-o-Nahaw, Mantiq, Falsafa, Balaghat, Hayat,*

Tafseer-e-Quran and the art of *Manazirah* are taught. The category of law and Jurisprudence consists of *Fiqh, Usool-e-Fiqh, Hadith, Usool-e-hadith, Aqeeda* etc.

Government of Uttar Pradesh Madrasa Board formulated structure of Madrasa education and its equivalent of modern education which is presented in the following Table No. 9.

Table 9

Kinds of Madaris and their Equivalence to Modern Education

Standard	*Class Level*	*Equivalent to*
Tahtania	Up to class V	Primary education
Foqania	VI-VIII	Middle education
Munshi/Maulvi	IX-X	Secondary/High School
Aalim	XI-XII	Intermediate/Senior Secondary School
Kamil	B.A	Graduate
Fazil	M.A	Post Graduate

Madaris, other than those affiliated to UP Madrasa Board, do not follow this structure of education. Non-affiliated Madaris do not necessarily follow uniform course structure and duration of study. Indeed, a non-affiliated Madrasa differs from another in its course structure and duration of a course.

Most of the 34 surveyed Madaris offer courses of *Tahtania* and *Foqania* level education. *Nazra* (Learning to read holy Quran without any understanding of Arabic language) is a course in 27 out of 34 Madaris. Duration of this course differs from a Madrasa to another. Its duration is one year in some Madaris and three years in others.

The course of *Hifz* (Memorization of the holy Quran), is offered by 19 Madaris. Only two Madaris offer the course of *Qirat* (stylish and lyrical method of reciting the holy Quran). The course of *Maulvi* is offered by four Madaris and that of *Munshi* is taught only in three Madaris. Both these courses are equivalent to IX and X level education. *Aalim/Alima* is a course equivalent to XI-XII class, which is offered by only five Madaris. Equivalent to graduation is the course of *Kamil* which exists only in two Madaris. Similar is the case with the course of *Fazil* which is equivalent to Post-graduation.

There are only two Madaris in which Arabic language is taught in the form of a structured course. In one Madrasa this course is taught as *Edadia* (Pre-primary level Arabic language) *Ula* (Class 1 level Arabic language) and *Sania* (Class 2 level Arabic language). While in another Madrasa, Arabic language is taught from a book called *Minahjul Arabia* which has 3-4 parts of elementary Arabic.

Talim-ul-Islam is the name of course formulated by Nadwatul Uloom, Lucknow, Uttar Pradesh which provides basic knowledge of Islamic tenets. This is offered by only one Madrasa and is of one-year duration. The course about fundamentals of Islam called *Deeniyat* is taught in two Madaris which is of two-year duration. Urdu, as a subject, is taught in four Madaris and only one Madrasa offers a course called *Usool-e-Aadad* (Elementary Arithmetic).

Table 10
Courses of Study in Madaris

Name of the Course	*Number of Madaris*
Nazra	27
Hifz	19
Munshi	03
Talim-ul-Islam	1
Urdu	4
Deeniyat	2
Edadia	1
Maulvi	4
Minhajul Arbia	1
Aalim/Alima	5
Usool-e-Aadad	1
Qirat	3
Sania	2
Ula	1
Kamil	2
Fazil	2

Madaris are not evenly distributed in villages and urban localities. Twenty-seven out of 34 are located in urban areas whereas 7 are found in villages. A village has two Madaris and remaining are distributed in 5 villages. Hence Madaris exist in six out of nine villages.

It is generally believed that Madaris are established only for boys and, therefore, girls are deprived of Madrasa education. Such a perception is fallacious by the findings of the survey. Indeed, five out of seven Madaris in villages are found co-educational. One is only for boys and another for only girls. Similarly, twenty out of twenty-seven Madaris of Aligarh city are co-educational whereas five are only for boys and remaining two are for only girls. In this way 25 out of 34 surveyed Madaris are co-educational and six are only for boys and three are only for girls. Hence girls and boys have equal access to Madrasa education.

Madrasa and Modern Education

Madrasa Modernization Scheme, launched by Government of India in 1993, aims at providing financial aid to Madaris for enabling them to introduce modern subjects such as Science, Mathematics, English etc., and improving their infrastructural facilities and quality of education. However, the benefits of this scheme have not been percolated down to each and every Madrasa. Despite having limited financial resources nine out of thirty-four surveyed Madaris have introduced modern subjects in their curriculum. This is shown in following Table No. 11.

Data in the Table No. 11 are self-explanatory. Nonetheless, respondents of remaining 25 Madaris are asked to give the reasons for not introducing modern subjects in their curriculum. Nineteen of them are in favour of introducing modern subjects in their curriculum but show their inability to do it because of following reasons:

- Lack of financial resources.
- No teacher of modern subject in Madrasa.
- Time constraint.

Three of the 25 respondents are not in favour of introducing modern subjects in Madaris. They think that it will divert the attention of students from Islamic education to modern education. Moreover, teaching of both Islamic and modern subjects will make students overburdened.

Table 11
Subjects of Modern Education in Sampled Madaris

Name of Madrasa	*Modern Subjects Offered*					
	Hindi	*English*	*Math*	*Science*	*So.Science*	*Computer*
Madrasa ArabiaTameer-e-Millat	Y	Y	Y	Y	Y	Y
Islamul Haq Madrasatul Banaat	Y	Y	Y	Y	Y	Y
Madrasa Islamia Arabia	Y	Y	Y	N	N	N
Lutfia Arabia	Y	Y	Y	Y	Y	Y
Siraj-ul-Uloom Niswan College	Y	Y	Y	Y	Y	N
Madrasa Jamia Darul Uloom Azizia	N	N	Y	N	N	N
Madrasatul Uloom Al Islamia	Y	Y	Y	Y	Y	Y
Madrasa Aqsa Talimul Quran	Y	Y	Y	N	N	N
Maqtab Nazmul Islam	Y	Y	Y	Y	Y	N

Y=Yes; N=No

Remaining three respondents did not report any reason for introducing modern subjects. In this way, majority of Madaris are in favour of introducing subjects of modern education in their curriculum. However, they are unable to introduce them mainly due to financial constraint.

Condition of Madrasa

Most of the Madaris have poor infrastructural facilities. They are deprived of required teaching staff and basic instructional/learning amenities like blackboards, classrooms, teaching aid material etc. Ten of the 34 Madaris are running from mosques where neither classrooms nor conducive atmosphere of instruction/learning are available. One of such Madaris is in a village whereas 9 are in Aligarh city. Another two Madaris are located in small houses and deprived of basic amenities. Remaining 22 Madaris exist in buildings, not attached with homes or mosque. However, 10 of such Madaris have buildings adjacent to mosques. Hence 12 Madaris may be described as having their independent buildings.

All Madaris except five have facility of drinking water whereas electricity is available in thirty Madaris. Toilet exists in 29 Madaris out of which only six have separate toilets for boys and girls. Small and rugged playgrounds are available only in thirteen Madaris. Merely three Madaris have computers which are intermittently used for students' training. Thus, Madaris suffer from several disadvantages. Yet, their significance cannot be undermined. Indeed, they are playing important role in promoting literacy and elementary education among children of poor families.

Financial Resources

One of the main reasons for impoverished condition of the Madaris is their limited financial resources. These Madaris function with charitable donations. *Zakat* (One of the five fundamentals of Islam, according to which a Muslim who has required amount of wealth is enjoined to pay two and half per cent of his/her assets annually for helping poor and destitute) and skin of sacrificed animals *(Charam Qurbani)* (A Muslim having required amount of wealth is enjoined to sacrifice animal on the 10th day of the last month of Islamic calendar) are collected for establishing a Madrasa and meeting its running costs. Besides, other charitable donation in cash and in kind are given by Muslims to Madaris. Information are sought from respondents about collection of various kinds of charities in last one year-2006. Twenty-three Madaris provided information in this regard which is presented in the following pages Table No. 12.

Government Aid to Muslim Managed Schools and Madaris

Government of India (GoI) launched various schemes for providing aid to minority educational institutions and creating educational infrastructure in minority concentration areas. Area Intensive Scheme (AIS) and Madrasa Modernization were two separate schemes, commenced in 1993 and later on merged into one scheme during Tenth Five Year Plan. AIS was started to provide basic infrastructure and facilities in areas where educationally backward minorities were concentrated, which do not have provisions for elementary and secondary education. Under the scheme, 100% financial assistance is provided to State Governments and the voluntary organizations for the following programmes:

- Establishment of new Primary/Upper Primary Schools, non-formal education centres where such a need is felt and viability established on the basis of a school mapping exercise.
- Strengthening of educational infrastructure and physical facilities in the Primary/ Upper Primary Schools.
- Opening of multi-stream residential Higher Secondary Schools for girls to impart studies in Science, Commerce, Humanities and Vocational courses.

Muslims, which had been covered under the umbrella of Educationally Backward Minorities, and Other Educationally Backward minorities, identified by States, were the target groups under the scheme.

Table 12
Charities to Madaris in 2006

Name of Madrasa	*Zakat*	*Skin of Sacrificed Animals*	*Income from Waqf Property*	*Other Donation*	*Total*
Madrasa Faizan-e-Mustafa	300,000	150,000	-	-	450,000
Madrasa Arabia Tameer-e-Millat	40,000	60,000	-	-	100,000
Madrasa Islamia Arabia	500	-	14,000	Rent of three houses	14,500
Dairatul Uloom	35,000	30,000	-	-	65,000
Madrasa Jamia Darul Uloom Azizia	8000	15000	-	-	23,000
Madrasatul Uloom Al Islamia	100,000	-	-	-	100,000
Madrasa Talimul Quran	-	1500	-	-	1,500
Madrasa Talimul Quran	15000	15000	-	-	30,000
Madrasa Hamidia Anwarul Uloom	-	5000	9,600	-	14,600
Gulabi Masjid Madrasa	-	2000	-	-	2,000
Mustafi Masjid wa Madrasa Talimul Islam	-	5000	-	1500	6,500
Madrasa Qasim-ul-Uloom	-	5000	-	-	5,000
Madrasa Reyaz Mustafa	-	3500	-	-	3,500
Madrasa Jamia Lutfia Qadiriya	1300	14000	-	-	15,300
Ek Tara Masjid & Madrasa Qadiriya	5000	17000	-	-	22,000
Madrasa Aqsa Talimul Quran	-	32000	-	8000	40,000
Islamia School/Madrasa	-	1000	-	-	1,000
Maktab Najmul Islam	-	2000	5,000	20,000	27,000

Contd.

Name of Madrasa	*Zakat*	*Skin of Sacrificed Animals*	*Income from Waqf Property*	*Other Donation*	*Total*
Madrasa Ansarul-Uloom,	-	-	3,300	No	3,300
Masjid Peer Ataullah	-	-	12,000	-	12,000
Madinatul Uloom	-	-	-	40,000	40,000
Madrasa Jamia Arabia Miftahul Uloom	-	-	20,000	9,000	29,000
Madrasa Arabia Darul Quran	-	-	-	800	800

Madrasa modernization aims at encouraging traditional institutions like Madaris and Maktabs by giving financial assistance to introduce Science, Mathematics, Social Studies, Hindi, and English in their curriculum. However, the process of modernization of traditional Madaris and Maktabs will be entirely voluntary. Indeed, primary aim of the scheme is to improve the standard of Madrasa education at par with the general education so that Muslim children studying in Madrasa may obtain education enabling them to compete in every walk of life.

Tehsil/block was the unit for the administration of the scheme. Initially the scheme was launched for 41 districts of the country. But the Ministry of Welfare was given the responsibility to identify more blocks/tehsil, districts on the basis of local conditions for more coverage. Ministry of Welfare, on the basis of 1981 Census data, identified 325 Tehsils/blocks of 89 districts spread over 13 states and 3 Union Territories for the implementation of the scheme. Tehsil Koil, District Aligarh, the universe of the survey, was identified as a unit for the implementation of the scheme. However, the scheme was not implemented in the Tehsil. There are other schemes of government of India providing aid to minority educational institutions. Hence we asked our respondents to provide information about the financial aid which they have received under any schemes of Government. Out of 65 Muslim managed schools, 13 have reported about receiving Government aid in the form of *wazifa* or scholarship to students. Some have received scholarship from the office of Basic Shiksha Adhikari (BSA) and others from District Minority Office. Merely four Madaris have reported about receiving the Government aid. Three of these Madaris namely, Madrasa Islamia Arabia, Siraj-ul-Uloom Niswan College and Madrasa Lutfia Arabia are receiving salaries of teachers from Uttar Pradesh Arabic-Persian Board. However, they have not disclosed amount of grant which they have received.

Madrasa Lutfia Arabia has also received kit under Madrasa Modernisation Scheme. Maktab Najmul Islam reported about receiving scholarship of Rs. 300/- per student per annum for 182 students from the office of BSA.

Thus most of the surveyed schools and Madaris are deprived of Government aid which they deserve to receive. This is mainly due to following reasons as per information of our respondents:

- Lack of information about Government schemes.
- Cumbersome bureaucratic procedure for receiving the aid.
- Officer's indifferent attitudes towards Muslim schools and Madaris.

7

Summary and Suggestions

Census of India did not provide detailed information about the status of Muslims and other religious communities of the country. Social scientists too did not pay much attention to the study of Indian Muslims. As a result, they remained hitherto little explored community. However, government committees/commissions attempted to gather quantitative information about the status of Muslims and other socio-religious communities. Since the data contained in these reports were macro in character, it was of little use to know micro level situation of Muslims. This survey was, therefore, conducted to explore the socio-economic and educational condition of Muslims in Tehsil Koil, District Aligarh.

Two thousand five hundred households were selected for the survey: one thousand from nine villages and fifteen hundred from twelve localities of three urban agglomerations namely Jalali, Pilakhna and Aligarh city. Also a survey of eighty-nine schools and thirty-four Madaris, located in surveyed localities, was conducted,

Of the total sampled households 66% were found simple and remaining complex. Merely 9.8% households were headed by females while remaining were male-headed. Nearly half of the households had *pucca* house and 29.24% lived in mixed house whereas 21% resided in *Kuchcha* houses and *'Jhopris'*.

Basic household amenities such as safe drinking water, electricity, and toilets were not available to all households. Twenty-seven per cent households did not have facility of drinking water within their houses whereas 66 per cent were deprived of electricity connection. Toilets were available to 58 per cent households and remaining used to go to open fields for defecation. Seven per cent households did not possess ration cards, an essential official document of a household identity. Merely 9 per cent households were issued Below Poverty Line (BPL) ration cards, though many more deserved for it.

Since selected households contained a population of 17,481 persons, average household size was of 7.0 persons, one point more than the district average (6.0). They had 925 females per 1000 males, 63 more than the district average. However, their WPR (22%), was 8 percentage points below to the district average. Distribution of 3926 workers according to their income and occupations revealed pathetic economic condition. Sixty-three per cent of workers had annual income upto rupees 2000/- whereas 30 per cent of them earned between rupees 2001/- to 5000/-. Income between rupees 5001/- to 10,000/- was of 5 per cent workers. Merely 1.35 per cent of them earned more than rupees 10,000/- per annum.

Occupations are more important than income in a hierarchical society like India. They define social status and affect life style of workers. Workers of selected households, found to be engaged in 52 occupations, were classified into four census categories of workers namely Cultivators, Agricultural Labourers, Household Industrial Workers and Other Workers. Estimate of this survey revealed 79 per cent Other Workers, 12.69 per cent Household Industrial Workers, 5.99 per cent Cultivators and 1.76 per cent Agricultural Labourers. Most of the workers were found to be associated with menial and irregular occupations which did not promise them regular and stable income.

Educational condition too was bad. Data exhibited 49 per cent average literacy rate among persons of 7 and above years age, nine percentage points below to the district average. It was 57 per cent and 40 percent among males and females respectively. Hence, 17 percentage points gender gap in literacy which was 11 percentage points below to district average.

Eighty-five per cent literates acquired 'Only Modern' education whereas merely 3.36 were 'Only Madrasa' educated. Remaining (11.37 per cent) were found having both 'Madrasa and Modern' education.

The phenomenon of decreasing numbers with increasing level of education prevailed in both Madrasa and Modern education. Forty-five per cent were found having merely Primary level education. The percentage sharply declined to 17.43 at Junior level education and remained consistently declining at all level of education. It was just 1.33 per cent at Post-graduate level. Only 135 persons were reported to have technical/professional education. Most of them acquired certificate/diploma level education.

A survey of 89 schools, located in surveyed localities and in their adjoining Muslim concentration habitation, revealed that 60 were only Primary (from Class I-V)) level schools, while 21 were Primary with Upper Primary (from Class I-VIII) standard. Yet another 6 schools imparted education to students from class VI to class VIII (Only Upper Primary). Merely two schools were of Secondary and Senior Secondary level education. All were private schools except 13 only Primary and 5 only Upper Primary Government schools. The quality of education in both Government and private schools was found below standard. Thus, neither Muslim children had access to schools of quality education nor did they have adequate facility of Secondary and Senior Secondary education. Educational condition of Muslims of Tehsil Koil may aptly be described in the words of PHLC 2006 which stated: "Muslims are at double disadvantage with low level of education combined with low quality of education; their deprivation increases manifold as the level of education rises".

Rural households appeared more deprived than urban households on all indicators of development. Twenty-seven percent of them as against 16 percent of urban households resided in *Kuchcha* houses and *Jhopris*. Facility of drinking water existed in 60 per cent rural and 80 per cent urban households. Similarly, 34 per cent of former and 74 per cent of the latter had toilets within homes. A marginal gap of three percentage points existed between rural (32%) and urban (35%) households in electricity connections. Likewise, WPR in villages (22%) was one percentage point below to urban areas. Seventy-one per cent workers of villages as against 58 per cent of urban areas belonged to lowest income ladder. Negligible i.e. 0.37 per cent workers of the former and two per cent workers of the latter categories figured in the highest income group. Similarly, literacy rate was 45 per cent in villages and 51 per cent in urban areas. Indeed, villagers lagged behind town dwellers at all level of education.

Muslims are not homogeneous community. They are internally divided into 'status groups' called *Baradaries*. Thirty-two different *Baradaries* were reported by Respondents. Twenty-four of them figured either in the Central or State List of OBCs and thus, remaining 8 included in General category. One thousand seven hundred fifty four households came from *Baradaries* of OBC category whereas 726 households belonged to *Baradaries* of General category. Twenty Respondents did not report their *Baradaries*. Administrative classification of *Baradaries* into General and OBCs and awareness about it is of vital importance. For Central and State governments initiated various policies and programmes for the welfare and empowerment of the latter category. However, majority of the Respondents did not know administrative status of their *Baradaries*. Merely 50% Respondents of General category and 26% of OBCs were found having correct awareness about administrative status of *Baradaries*.

Muslim OBCs appeared more deprived than Muslim General in the sphere of economy and education. For example, 57 per cent workers of General category as against 65 per cent of OBC came from lowest income group. Although their percentage in the second income group was almost equal (29.58% General and 30.35% OBCs), disparity of income between them persisted in the third (8.95% General and 3.63% OBCs) and in the highest income group (3.54% General and 0.44% OBCs). Similarly, Muslim OBCs lagged behind Muslim Generals in both traditional and modern higher education.

Thus, Muslims are entrenched into vicious circle of backwardness which mainly emanate from their social composition and insecurity as well as lack of effective government and voluntary intervention for them. Sociologically, Muslims are composed of different hierarchically placed *Baradaries*, broadly classified into three categories i.e. *Ashraf, Ajlaf* and *Arzal. Ashraf*, meaning noble, includes all Muslims of foreign blood and converts from higher castes. They constituted uppermost echelon of Muslim social structure in the past. Among them were *zamindars, jagirdars*, scholars, administrators, military men etc. who experienced sudden downfall in their socio-economic and political status just immediately after the partition of the country due to migration to Pakistan, abolition of *zamindari* and deprivation of state employment. While *Ajlaf*, meaning degraded or unholy, consists of ritually clean occupational groups and low ranking converts. *Arzal* contains *Baradaries* of lowest status, traditionally associated with ritually unclean occupations. About 70% Muslim population is of *Ajlaf* and *Arzal* who have been engaged in low paid menial occupations and dispossessed of physical asset and education.

It is obvious that such an underprivileged community cannot keep pace with others in a competitive and democratic society without having free and fair atmosphere and effective State's support. Muslims have virtually been deprived of both. India has not yet provided safety and security to their life and property. Thousands of Muslims are killed, women are raped and their hard-earned valuable properties as well as economic bases are razed to the ground in frequently occurring organized and very often politically supported violence against them in post independent India. Growing insecurity to their life and property push them to live in ghettoes or in seclusion from main stream society. Their areas of concentration are deprived of civic amenities and economic opportunities. They fear to send their children to educational institutions and open their business establishment in non-Muslim areas. In this way, they have been deprived of developmental benefits.

Inclusion of excluded communities is the goal of Indian Constitution. Hence policy of reservation and welfare schemes are framed to bring Scheduled Castes, Scheduled Tribes and Other Backward Classes into national mainstream. But Muslims have not been benefited from these policies which radically transformed socio-economic and political status of non-Muslim communities. The policy of reservation excludes Muslims from Scheduled Caste, though many communities of Muslims like *Arzals* deserve to be included in it. Status of Scheduled Tribes has not been accorded to many Muslim communities, living in forest and remote areas and having socio-economic condition similar to non-Muslim tribals. For example, while Hindu Minas are recognized as tribes, Muslim Meos/Mewati have been deprived of the status despite the fact both Minas and Mewatis have similar social origin. Although Muslim *Ajlaf* are included in the list of OBCs, they are unable to get the benefit of reservation policy and welfare schemes because many of them are poor and illiterate and do not even know administrative status of their Baradaries. They are unable to compete with economically prosperous and politically powerful non-Muslim OBCs. In this way, Muslims have virtually been placed out of reservation and welfare policies network. Benefits of minorities' welfare schemes too have not reached to them. Indeed, Government of India did not launch specific programme for the welfare of minorities until 1980s. Few insubstantial schemes for their welfare were framed in the last two decades. However, evidences show that schemes were not implemented with sincerity and commitment.

Thus, Muslims, being largely composed of *Ajlaf* and *Arzals*, subjected to continuous violence and insecurity, forced to live in ghettoes and deprived of State's support, have reduced to lowest ebb of Indian society. Their condition cannot be improved unless (a) the quality of their educational institutions is improved and facilities of education and civic amenities are created in localities of their concentration (b) they are provided safety of their life and property as well as multiple effective State's intervention for their uplift (c) they are given due representation in power structure and State employment. They should immediately be given reservation as recommended by

Rangnath Mishra Committee in education and employment (d) States are legally enjoined to implement minorities welfare schemes in time and (e) an organized powerful movement of voluntary action should be initiated among them.

References

Census (2001), *Census of India 2001: Report on Religion Data (Series 10:Uttar Pradesh)*. Lucknow: Joint Director, Directorate of Census Operation, Uttar Pradesh and Uttranchal.

GOI (2006), *Social, Economic and Educational Status of the Muslim Community of India- A Report*. New Delhi: Prime Minister's High Level Committee, Cabinet Secretariat, Government of India (Chairperson Justice Rajindar Sachar).

GOI (2007), *The National Commission for Religious and Linguistic Minorities-A Report*, New Delhi: Ministry of Minority Affairs (Chairperson Justice Ranganath Mishra, Former Chief Justice of India).

Ansari, G. (1960), *Muslim Caste in Uttar Pradesh: A Study of Cultural Contact*. Lucknow: The Ethnographic and Folk Cultural Society, U.P.

Ahmad, Imtiaz (1973), *Caste and Social Stratification Among Muslims in India*, New Delhi: Manohar

Mann, E.A. (1992), *Boundaries and Identities: Muslim Work and Status in Aligarh*. New Delhi: Sage Publishers India Pvt. Ltd.

Annexures

Annexure - I

Map of Uttar Pradesh

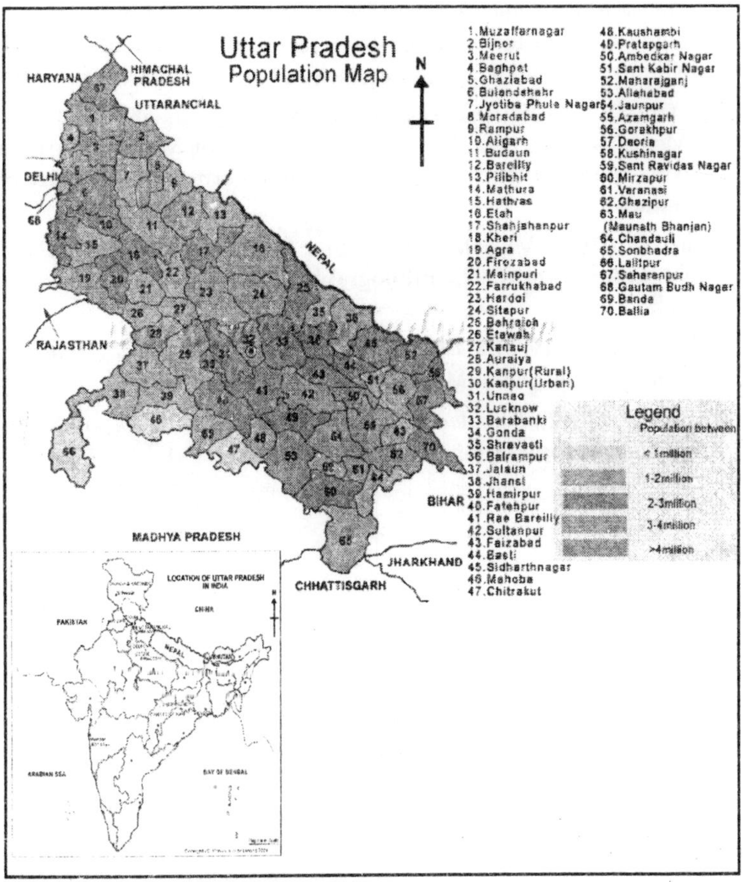

Annexure - II
Map of Aligarh

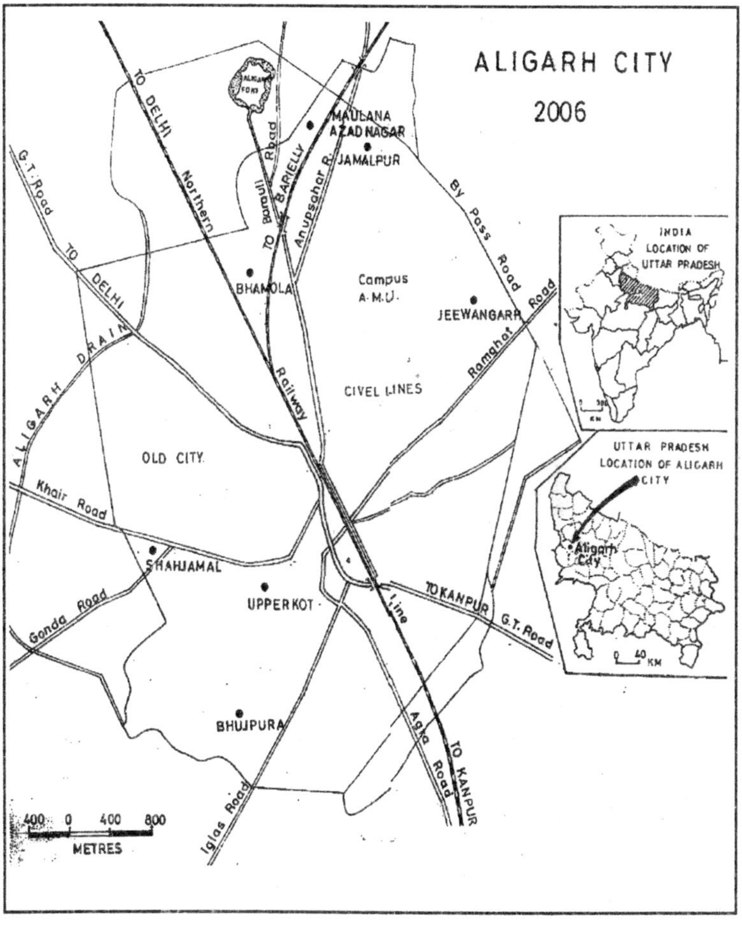

Annexure-III

List of Government, Muslim and Non-Muslim Managed Schools in Surveyed Localities

Name of School	Name of the Village/ Locality	Ph.No.	Block/ Nagar Mahapalika	Year of Establishment	Establishment Status: Lowest Class at Establishment	Establishment Status: Highest Class at Establishment	Present Status: Lowest Class in School at Present	Present Status: Highest Class in School at Present	Registration	Recognition	Govt	Pvt.: Muslim Managed	Pvt.: Non-Muslim Managed
Alda Public School	Jeevangarh	9897520401	Aligarh	1984	Nursery	5	Nursery	8	Yes	Yes		Yes	
Alfia Pub. School	Shahjamal		Aligarh	2001	1	5	1	5	Yes	Yes		Yes	
Al-Hadi Public School	Bhamola	9219613695	Aligarh	2007	Nursery	5	Nursery	5	No	Yes		Yes	
Ali Primary School	Badam Nagar	9358216317	Aligarh	2001	Nursery	KG	Nursery	5	Yes	Yes		Yes	
Ali Pub. School	Shahjamal	9837848481	Aligarh	1996	Nursery	5	Nursery	5	Yes	Yes		Yes	
Aligarh Muslim School	Tantan Para, Upper fort	9358090504	Aligarh	1986	6	6	6	8	Yes	Yes		Yes	
Allama Public School	Mushtaq Nagar	0571-2407243	Aligarh	2002	Nursery	5	Nursery	5	Yes	Yes		Yes	
Ansar Girls Pub. School	Jeevangarh	9719899866	Aligarh	2001	Nursery	5	Nursery	8	Yes	Yes		Yes	
Ayesha Modern Pub School	Barola Jafrabad	9219300778	Lodha	2005	Nursery	8	Nursery	8	Yes	No		Yes	
Ayesha Pub School	Zohrabagh		Aligarh	1998	Nursery	5	Pre-Nursery	8	Yes	Yes		Yes	
Azad Public School	Jamalpur	9410692889	Aligarh	1997	Nursery	5	Nursery	8	Yes	Yes		Yes	
City Public School	Bhamola		Aligarh	1989	Nursery	8	Nursery	8	Yes	Yes		Yes	
Daffodils Public School	Bhamola	9759475174	Aligarh	2001	Nursery	5	Nursery	8	Yes	Yes		Yes	
Dream Hills Convent School	Rorawar	9359512211	Aligarh	2006	Nursery	6	Nursery	6	Yes	No		Yes	
Ekta Pri. Girls School	Jeevangarh	9719899866	Aligarh	2001	Nursery	5	Nursery	5	Yes	Yes		Yes	
Evergreen Montessori School	Bhamola	9219146662	Aligarh	2006	Nursery	1	Nursery	1	Yes	Yes		Yes	
Expert Public School	Bhamola	9358604213	Aligarh	2006	Nursery	5	Nursery	5	Yes	Yes			Yes
Fatima Mod. School	Jamalpur	9897531953	Aligarh	1996	Nursery	5	Nursery	5	Yes	Yes		Yes	
Girl Junior High School	Jalali		Dhanipur		6	8	1	8	No	Yes	Yes		
Glorious Pub. School	ADA Colony	0571-2511601	Aligarh	2003	Nursery	6	Nursery	8	Yes	Yes		Yes	
Green Garden Public School	Jamalpur	9358372669	Aligarh	2006	Nursery	5	Nursery	5	Yes	Yes		Yes	

Contd.

Name of School	Name of the Village/ Locality	Ph.No.	Block/ Nagar Mahapalika	Year of Establishment	Establishment Status: Lowest Class at Establishment	Establishment Status: Highest Class at Establishment	Present Status: Lowest Class in School at Present	Present Status: Highest Class in School at Present	Registration	Recognition	Govt.	Pvt.: Muslim Managed	Pvt.: Non-Muslim Managed
H.M.S. Public School	Bhamola	9897763884	Aligarh	1999	Nursery	5	Nursery	5	Yes	Yes		Yes	
Habib Mem. Pub. School	Jeevangarh	9319903621	Aligarh	2006	Nursery	4	Nursery	5	No	Yes		Yes	
Habib Mem. Pub. School	Bhamola	0571-2325303	Aligarh	2001	Nursery	2	Nursery	4	Yes	Yes		Yes	
Heritage Pub. School	Rorawar		Aligarh	2007	Nursery	5	Nursery	5	No	No			Yes
Indian Public School	Jamalpur	9719413770	Aligarh	2000	Nursery	5	Nursery	5	Yes	Yes		Yes	
Indian Public School	Pilakhana	93581787244	Pilakhna	2006	1	5	1	5	Yes	Yes		Yes	
Indian Sunrise Public School	Nai Basti	9319879755	Aligarh	2005	Nursery	5	Nursery	5	Yes	No		Yes	
Indra Public School	Sarai Rehman	9897430257	Aligarh	1998	Nursery	5	Nursery	5	Yes	No		Yes	
Indus Pub. School	Jamalpur	9897180241	Aligarh	2002	Nursery	5	Nursery	8	Yes	Yes		Yes	
Ishrat pub. Jun. High School	ADA Colony	0571-2520798	Aligarh	1997	Nursery	5	Nursery	8	Yes	Yes		Yes	
Islamia Girls School	Sarai Rehman	0571-2523547	Aligarh	1991	Nursery	8	Nursery	8	No	Yes		Yes	
Islamia Montessori Pri. School	Sarai Rehman	9358354663	Aligarh	1994	Nursery	1	Nursery	5	Yes	Yes		Yes	
Islamia Nursery School	Tantan Para, Upper fort	9358090504	Aligarh	1971	Nursery	2	Nursery	5	Yes	Yes		Yes	
Islamia Urdu Maktab	Jalali		Jalali	1927	1	5	KG	5	Yes	Yes		Yes	
Jagat Singh Tyagi High School	Sarai Rehman	9412272359	Aligarh	1965	1	8	1	10	Yes	Yes			Yes
Jai Kisan Pub School	Brahmana	9358178761	Pilakhna	1995	Nursery	4	Nursery	5	Yes	Yes			Yes
Junior High School	Chandpur Mirza		Akrabad	1993	6	8	6	8	No	Yes	Yes		
Junior High School,	Ilyaspur		Lodha	2004	6	8	6	8	Yes	Yes	Yes		
Junior High School,	Talaspur Khurd		Lodha	2005	6	6	6	7	No	No	Yes		
Junior School	Nanau		Akrabad	1975	6	8	6	8	No	Yes	Yes		
K.B.Memorial Islamia Public School	Jamalpur	9219893658	Aligarh	2003	Nursery	5	Nursery	5	Yes	Yes		Yes	
K.U. Pub. School	Jangal gari		Aligarh	1997	Nursery	5	Nursery	5	Yes	Yes		Yes	
Khan Pub. School	Shahganj	9219956400	Aligarh	1993	Nursery	5	Nursery	5	Yes	Yes		Yes	
Kids Island Basic Academy	Hamdard Nagar	9897266927	Aligarh	2001	Nursery	5	Nursery	8	Yes	Yes		Yes	
Little Star Public School	Bhamola	2701801	Aligarh	2006	Nursery	8	Nursery	8	Yes	No		Yes	

Contd.

Name of School	Name of the Village/ Locality	Ph.No.	Block/ Nagar Mahapalika	Year of Establis-hment	Establishment Status: Lowest Class at Establis-hment	Establishment Status: Highest Class at Establis-hment	Present Status: Lowest Class in School at Present	Present Status: Highest Class in School at Present	Regis-tration	Recog-nition	Govt.	Pvt.: Muslim Managed	Pvt.: Non-Muslim Managed
Lucent Public School	Upper Fort	9319889996	Aligarh	2006	Nursery	3	Nursery	3	No	No		Yes	
Lutfia Inter College	Upper Fort	0571-2522868	Aligarh	1968	6	8	1	12	Yes	Yes		Yes	
M.I.M. Pub School	Akrabad	9927156104	Akrabad	2006	Nursery	8	Nursery	8	No	No		Yes	
M.R.Pub.School	Hamdard Nagar	9358203311	Aligarh	2002	Nursery	3	Nursery	3	No	No		Yes	
M.S. Pub School	Shahganj		Aligarh	2003	Nursery	5	Nursery	5	Yes	No		Yes	
Maktab Islamia	Pilakhana	9719042929	Pilakhna	1933	1	5	1	5	Yes	Yes		Yes	
Maulana Azad Junior High School	Jamalpur		Aligarh	1993	Nursery	5	Nursery	8	Yes	Yes		Yes	
Maulana Azad Memorial School	Sarai Rehman	9897865730	Aligarh	1993	Nursery	5	Nursery	5	Yes	Yes		Yes	
Modern Ideal Public School	Bhamola	9837667299	Aligarh	2000	Nursery	8	Nursery	5	Yes	Yes		Yes	
Moon Public School	Jamalpur, Hamdard Nagar	0571-3250178	Aligarh	2000	Nursery	5	Nursery	5	Yes	Yes		Yes	
Mughis Memorial School	Sarai Rehman	0571-2407189	Aligarh	2006	Nursery	5	Nursery	5	No	Yes		Yes	
Mumtaz Pub. School	Teipada	9927881889	Aligarh	1992	Nursery	5	Nursery	5	No	Yes		Yes	
Mumtaz Pub. School	Rorawar	9927881889	Aligarh	2006	Nursery	5	Nursery	5	No	Yes		Yes	
Munirul Uloom Pri. School	Rorawar		Aligarh	2006	Nursery	5	Nursery	5	No	No		Yes	
Muslim Public School	Jamalpur	9412816974	Aligarh	1987	Nursery	2	Nursery	2	Yes	Yes		Yes	
N.U. Pub. School	Jeevangarh	9358203311	Aligarh	1997	Nursery	2	Nursery	5	No	Yes		Yes	
National Pub High School	Jeevangarh	9412597417	Aligarh	2001	Nursery	5	Nursery	8	Yes	Yes		Yes	
Nida Pub. School	Jeevangarh		Aligarh	2001	Nursery	3	Nursery	5	Yes	No		Yes	
Nisar Public School	Jeevangarh		Aligarh	2007	Nursery	4	Nursery	4	Yes	No		Yes	
Non-Residential Bridge Course School	Jalali		Jalali	2007	1	3	1		No	Yes		Yes	
Paras Pub. School	Rorawar	9319515216	Aligarh	2003	Nursery	5	Nursery	5	Yes	No		Yes	
Play and Learn Public School	Bani Israilane	0571-253586	Aligarh	1994	Nursery	KG	Nursery	8	Yes	Yes		Yes	
Primary Pathshala No.1	Jalali		Jalali	1936	1	5	1	5	Yes	Yes	Yes		

Contd.

Name of School	Name of the Village/ Locality	Ph.No.	Block/ Nagar Mahapalika	Year of Establishment	Establishment Status: Lowest Class at Establishment	Establishment Status: Highest Class at Establishment	Present Status: Lowest Class in School at Present	Present Status: Highest Class in School at Present	Registration	Recognition	Govt.	Pvt.: Muslim Managed	Pvt.: Non-Muslim Managed
Primary School	Nanau		Akrabad	1999	1	5	1	5	No	Yes	Yes		
Primary School	Faridpur	9837125415	Dhanipur	2003	1	5	1	5	No	Yes	Yes		
Primary School	Talaspur Khurd		Lodha	1979	1	5	1	5	No	Yes	Yes		
Primary School	Ilyaspur		Lodha	1994	1	2	1	5	No	Yes	Yes		
Primary School	Chandpur Mirza		Akrabad	1993	1	5	1	5	No	Yes	Yes		
Primary School No. 50, (Boys)	Bhujpura		Aligarh	1960	1	5	1	5	No	Yes	Yes		
Primary School No.1	Akrabad		Akrabad	1960	1	5	1	5	No	Yes	Yes		
Primary School No.2	Jalali		Dhanipur	1971	1	5	1	5	Yes	No	Yes		
Primary School No.2	Akrabad		Akrabad	1998	1	5	1	5	No	Yes	Yes		
Primary School No.35 Girls	Jangal gari		Aligarh	1960	1	5	1	5	No	Yes	Yes		
Primary School No.35,	Jaiganj		Aligarh	1945	1	5	1	5	No	Yes	Yes		
Raj National Pub. School	Jamalpur	9897453272	Aligarh	2001	Nursery	5	Nursery	5	Yes	Yes		Yes	
Raza Public School	Hamdard Nagar	9319399414	Aligarh	1997	Nursery	5	Nursery	8	Yes	Yes		Yes	
Rising Public School	Jamalpur		Aligarh	2000	Nursery	4	Nursery	5	Yes	Yes		Yes	
S. K. Public School	Jaiganj	0571-2410767	Aligarh	1996	Nursery	5	Nursery	8	Yes	Yes		Yes	
Salmania Pri. School	Upper Fort	0571-2513665	Aligarh	1980	Nursery	5	Nursery	5	Yes	Yes		Yes	
Setu Siksha Kendra	Chappar Wali Masjid	9719253462	Aligarh	1989	1	5	1	5	Yes	Yes			Yes
Shivaji Siksha Niketan	Pilakhana	9411628028	Pilakhna	2001	LKG	3	LKG	5	Yes	Yes			Yes
Sir Syed Junior High School	Jamalpur		Aligarh	1991	Nursery	5	Nursery	8	Yes	Yes		Yes	
Warsi Public School	Jamalpur		Aligarh	1999	Nursery	5	Nursery	5	Yes	Yes		Yes	

Annexure-IV
List of Madaris

Name of Madrasa	*Complete Address*	*Nature of Madrasa*	*Madrasa Type*
Madrasa Jamia Arabia Miftahul Uloom	Talaspur Khurd, Lodha	Boys	Home Based
Markaz Uloomun Nisa	Chandpur Mirza, Akrabad	Co-ed	Independent Structure
Madrasa Hamidia Anwarul Uloom	Shisgram, Akrabad, Akrabad	Co-ed	Independent Structure
Madrasa Madina Masjid	Dhanipur, Adhon, Dhanipur	Co-ed	At Mosque
Madrasa-e-Arabia Bilalia	Dhanipur, Adhon, Dhanipur	Girl's	Independent Structure
Islamia School/Madrasa	Faridpur, Jullupur Sinhor, Dhanipur	Co-ed	Independent Structure
Maktab Najmul Islam	Chandpur Mirza, Akrabad	Co-ed	Independent Structure
Madarsâ Faizan-e-Mustafa	Zohra Bagh, Nai Abadi, Aligarh	Co-ed	Independent Structure but linked with Mosque
Madrasa Arabia Tameer-e-Millat	Gosht wali Gali, Dodhpur, Aligarh	Boys	Independent Structure but linked with Mosque
Madrasa Anwar Masjid (Bari Masjid)	S.S. Nagar, Aligarh	Boys	Independent Structure but linked with Mosque
Islamul Haq Madrasatul Banaat	Near Bari Masjid, S.S. Nagar, Aligarh	Girl's	Independent Structure
Madrasa Islamia Arabia	Jama Masjid, Upper Fort, Aligarh	Boys	Independent Structure but linked with Mosque
Lutfia Arabia	Tantan Para, Upper Fort, Aligarh	Co-ed	Independent Structure
Madrasa Ansarul-Uloom	Masjid Boo Ali Shah, Aligarh	Co-ed	At Mosque
Masjid Peer Ataullah	Upper Fort,Aligarh	Co-ed	At Mosque
Siraj-ul-Uloom Niswan College	Gali Sheikhain, Upper Fort, Aligarh	Girl's	Independent Structure
Dairatul Uloom	Tantan Para, Upper Fort, Aligarh	Co-ed	Independent Structure
Madrasa Jamia Darul Uloom Azizia	Super Colony, Bhojpura, Aligarh	Boys	Independent Structure but linked with Mosque
Madinatul Uloom	Siraj Nagar, Bhojpura, Aligarh	Co-ed	Independent Structure but linked with Mosque
Madrasa Mujaddadi Hifz wa Tajvidul Quran	Bari Masjid, Taar Wali Gali, Sarai Rehman,Aligarh	Co-ed	Independent Structure
Madrasa Talimul Quran	Masjid Gulabi Jadid Loco Colony, Nai Abadi, Gali No. 15, Aligarh	Co-ed	At Mosque
Madrasa Talimul Quran	Zohra Bagh Chauraha, Aligarh	Co-ed	Independent Structure but linked with Mosque
Madrasa Talimul Quran	Jama Masjid, Bhamola, Aligarh	Co-ed	At Mosque
Mustafai Masjid wa Madrasa Talimul Islam	Gali No. 2, Loco Nai Abadi, Aligarh	Co-ed	Independent Structure but linked with Mosque
Madrasa Qasim-ul-Ulcom	Zakir Nagar, Main Road Jeevangarh Aligarh	Co-ed	At Mosque

Contd.

Name of Madrasa	*Complete Address*	*Nature of Madrasa*	*MadrasaType*
Madrasa Reyaz Mustafa	Gali No. 10, Jeevangarh,Aligarh	Co-ed	Independent Structure
Madrasa Jamia Lutfia Qadiriya	Gali No.1, Abbas Nagar, Jeevangarh Aligarh	Co-ed	At Mosque
Ek Tara Masjid & Madrasa Qadiriya	Gali No. 3, Jeevengarh, Aligarh	Co-ed	At Mosque
Madrasa Arabia Darul Quran	Purani Eidgah, Shahjamal, Aligarh	Co-ed	At Mosque
Faizul Quran Maktab	Hazrat Bilali Masjid, Shahjamal, Aligarh	Co-ed	At Mosque
Madrasa Aqsa Talimul Quran	Gali No.5, Shahjamal, Shahjamal Aligarh	Co-ed	Independent Structure
Mazharul Uloom	Bhamola, Alam Bagh, Aligarh	Co-ed	Home Based
Madrasatul Uloom Al Islamia	Hamdard nagar 'D', Jamalpur, Aligarh	Boys	Independent Structure but linked with Mosque
Gulabi Masjid Madrasa	Gali No.13, Nai Abadi, Loco Colony Aligarh	Co-ed	Independent Structure but linked with Mosque
Madrasa Qasim-ul-Uloom	Zakir Nagar, Main Road Jeevangarh Aligarh	Co-ed	At Mosque
Madrasa Reyaz Mustafa	Gali No. 10, Jeevangarh,Aligarh	Co-ed	Independent Structure
Madrasa Jamia Lutfia Qadiriya	Gali No.1, Abbas Nagar, Jeevangarh Aligarh	Co-ed	At Mosque
Ek Tara Masjid & Madrasa Qadiriya	Gali No. 3, Jeevengarh, Aligarh	Co-ed	At Mosque
Madrasa Arabia Darul Quran	Purani Eidgah, Shahjamal, Aligarh	Co-ed	At Mosque
Faizul Quran Maktab	Hazrat Bilali Masjid, Shahjamal, Aligarh	Co-ed	At Mosque
Madrasa Aqsa Talimul Quran	Gali No.5, Shahjamal, Shahjamal Aligarh	Co-ed	Independent Structure
Mazharul Uloom	Bhamola, Alam Bagh, Aligarh	Co-ed	Home Based
Madrasatul Uloom Al Islamia	Hamdard nagar 'D', Jamalpur, Aligarh	Boys	Independent Structure but linked with Mosque